YOUR SOUL MATE AWAITS!

YOUR SOUL MATE AWAITS!

A Matchmaker Reveals
How to
Find Love and Happiness in
3 Simple Steps

Judith Gottesman, M.S.W.

With Maria De La O

Judith Gottesman
SoulMatesUnlimited.com

ISBN: 979-8-9850911-0-6
Library of Congress Control Number: 2021921093

** All client names and identifying details have been changed to protect privacy.*

This book is dedicated in memory of my father,
Rabbi Aaron Gottesman, and to all those
looking for love who won't give up hope
that their soul mate is out there.

CONTENTS

Love is not quantifiable; it doesn't generate doomed statistics. It is ignored in policy debates. And yet, in the end, love is the source of all our meaningful values.

— Sam Anderson, in his *New York Times* story
"The Last Two Northern White Rhinos on Earth"

PREFACE

I've had varying job titles in my adult years, some ordinary, some anything but. I was a geriatric social worker that coordinated a program for low-income Holocaust survivors. I worked as a marketing consultant. I had my own pet-sitting business, and I was a religious school teacher and an education director. I traipsed around the Venezuelan rainforest as a research assistant studying capuchin monkey behavior, and I even had a short stint as Cyndi Lauper's personal assistant's assistant. Throughout all, however, there was one thing I always did, not for pay, but for the good deed — and that was matchmaking.

After many years of unofficial matchmaking, the first match I officially made was for a friend who lived in Montreal in the late 1990s, when I lived in New York City. I wanted to set her up with someone I knew in New York, but it took six months until I could have them meet — since they were both in relationships when I first thought of them for each other. I was sure they were soul mates, and told my friend to let me know when she was single again.

After a few months, as I predicted, she broke up with her boyfriend. Soon after, she visited me in New York, so I called the guy and had him arrange the date. They went out, and even though they had a nice time, my Canadian friend was less than impressed with the way he ended the date. I pushed her to go out with him a second time, and as they say, the rest is history. They are now both in New York, on faculty at a top university, and very happily married with two kids. I learned from them that it's worth waiting for matches to happen, and also that sometimes love isn't always at first sight. People often have a difficult time recognizing their soul mates, letting fear or preconceived ideas of how someone should act on a phone call or date block their ability to be open to a person who is perfect for them.

I went on to set up other couples I was sure were soul mates over the years, all of whom got married and are still happily married. I discovered that I have an intuitive sense and was good at somehow recognizing soul mates, even if one person was someone I just met or didn't know well. And I was never wrong. Every single person I had that "soul mate feeling" about got married. Every person who is married through me married the very first person I set them up with.

Whenever people heard I had an "intuition" for matchmaking, they always wanted me to find a match for themselves or their friends. So many people were asking for my assistance, I finally decided to officially go into business as a professional matchmaker on a full-time basis.

"Oh, you're a yenta!" people will often say when meeting me. "Actually, no," I reply. "I'm not a yenta." A yenta is seen as a gossipy woman, while the correct Hebrew term for a

Jewish matchmaker is actually *shadchanit* for a woman and *shadchan* for a man. To me, a yenta has a negative connotation. She's the character on *Fiddler on the Roof* who was sort of a nosy, busybody type, and not necessarily the best skilled at matchmaking. (Although I'll definitely call or email the parties to remind them it's really important they follow up when I have a really strong sense that two people should meet each other. Does that make me a busybody?)

Now, when people find out I'm a matchmaker, they stop me on the street walking my dog or at parties, in restaurant bathrooms, on airplanes (our conversations usually last the entire flight), in the pool locker room — really anywhere you can imagine. They want to talk about what I do, and see what I think of them if they're a couple, or find out if I have a match for them if they're single. No other job I've had has evoked such interested reactions from people. (I guess it's a little like saying you're a doctor. Everyone wants to ask you about their symptoms and tell you their entire medical histories.) It's incredible how total strangers share the details of their lives, whether it's worries about their single adult child, personal dating woes, or the nitty-gritty of their divorces. There are even some rare ones who tell me about their happy marriages.

My father, Rabbi Aaron Gottesman, performed lots of weddings and I grew up attending many of them. He would always cite meaningful and romantic personal anecdotes as part of the ceremony. My father did a lot of premarital and couples counseling, too. I used to talk to him about what made happy couples and what were causes of conflict. Maybe that was the spark of my lifelong interest in love.

As a former social worker, I now believe there's no more effective form of social work than helping people find love. Nothing makes life better than love. Nothing. Even with difficulties such as health or financial problems, having someone to love makes these challenges seem surmountable rather than hopeless. People who have a loving support system live longer and are healthier overall, compared with people who are alone. And couples are typically better off financially than singles, if only because they can share costs and have dual incomes. I'm fortunate to be in a profession that allows me to profoundly change people's lives for the better.

But let me let you in on a little secret. You don't need to hire a professional matchmaker to find love. My job is really about seeing the possibilities that people may not see on their own, helping them break through their own psychological barriers, and guiding and cheerleading them through the dating process — all pieces of the puzzle that, if used correctly, this book can facilitate too. By using the simple steps and the techniques I outline here, you really can do it on your own, though it's always good to have a matchmaker like myself keeping you in mind for potentials as well.

I know. You feel like your life is full. You're happy, you have a nice circle of close friends, a successful career, and your weekends are full of socializing and volunteer work. So why do you need a romantic partner? Not everyone does. But you are reading this book, so clearly you likely have an interest in sharing your fabulous life with someone.

Many people who talk to me about my services as a matchmaker start out on the defensive. They feel like they need to tell me how wonderful they are and how full their lives are, despite the fact that they are single or divorced or widowed. I always tell them that this is the perfect time to come to me. When you're satisfied with your full life and feel good about yourself, it's the perfect time to attract love into your life. After all, who wants to come to your party if it isn't any fun?

That's where this book comes in. The intention is not just to help you to find a mate; to attract your soul mate, the work starts way before that. If your life is great, you're already on your way. I'll just help you to get in the right mental framework and give you action steps to find that special someone. If, conversely, your life could use some improvement, I'll help you improve and reframe that too, to put you in the right orbit for love. Soul mate matches are special and rare. If they weren't, no one would be single and no one would be divorced. As a matchmaker, I take all of my potential matches very personally and I am invested in my clients' success — whether it's someone I've worked with personally or a "client" who's simply reading this book. When I see a soul mate match that I helped create come to be, it's the most satisfying and thrilling feeling to know I had a hand in greatly changing these two people's lives for the better.

Through my work as a matchmaker, I've come to believe that finding one's soul mate can be distilled into *three distinct steps.*

First on the list is ***Desire.*** You must genuinely desire a romantic partner if you're going to invite one into your life. Now this may seem obvious, but believe me, not everyone who comes to me truly desires a partner with their heart and soul. They may simply believe instead that they "should" have a mate — not at all the same thing, and an idea that may have more to do with familial or societal expectations than their deepest feelings. In fact, I'm contacted by a surprising number of parents and relatives who believe that their successful son, daughter, or other relative needs to find a wife or husband right away. I always reply that the potential clients need to want it and to contact me, themselves; that I can't find a match for someone based on a third party's say-so or desire for them.

Thus, the first part of this book will help you answer the question of desire for yourself.

Second is *Believe*. You must truly believe that there is someone out there for you and that you are capable of meeting and falling into a mutual love relationship with this person. It's a tall order, and not everyone has strong enough self-esteem to believe all of the above.

This is where we get serious! Belief focuses on inner work, and depending upon how much of it you've already done, it can be a fairly straightforward task or the most difficult step in the process. I've been inspired in my thinking by Iyanla Vanzant's book *In the Meantime,* which is all about making the most of your life — living a full and meaningful existence as a single person, both because it makes you happy and because it helps attract your soul mate to be a part of the wonderful life you've created. In a similar vein, my book is meant to be a practical guide to give you simple and direct steps to creating a life worth living — and sharing.

Third, and last on the list, is the ability to ***Act.*** While the first two steps help you to know yourself and what you want, they alone may or may not result in you finding your love match. If you're very lucky, of course they may be sufficient — after all, I'm sure that someone ended up marrying the cable guy who just happened to come by to install her television— but it's not a very sure-fire road to love.

Napoleon Hill, in *Think and Grow Rich,* calls for organized effort to achieve success, and recommends using Andrew Carnegie's "definiteness of purpose" in everything you do to help make your goal a reality. Just as you don't grow wealthy or achieve success at work or school without some sort of concerted, sustained effort, you are unlikely to hit the love jackpot with lazy, half-baked efforts at meeting people. (Although as in the cable guy example, chance meetings with no concerted effort will, of course, work out for a lucky few, but you'd be ill-advised on depending that they'll work out for you personally.) Therefore, the third step in my framework will give you the practical tools to purposefully turn your dreams of having a soul mate into reality.

Follow the steps in my program and you'll bring love into your life. You want to know how long it will take? You want assurances that it will take 30 days, or 90 days, or that by the end of the year you'll have your soul mate, like so many books promise? I don't believe we can will love into our lives on a time frame. The people that achieve their goal of marriage in six months, a year, or some similar set time frame are likely to have simply found someone looking to get married too — not necessarily a soul mate.

Simply being married isn't success. Anybody can be miserably married (or happily divorced, for that matter). Success is being in a happily committed relationship with your soul mate, a goal that is infinitely more difficult to achieve than marriage, but sweeter for it. If you believe in soul mates, you have to understand that there is a higher power in charge, and as long as you are open to love, you will wind up with the one you are meant to. You don't know the big picture; you only know your perspective in your current life.

Maybe you think you're ready for love, but you really aren't. My book will help get you there. Or maybe you are ready, but your soul mate isn't. He may be trekking the Himalayas for the next year, caring for an ill spouse for the next two years, or in the midst of a nasty divorce and custody battle, which will play out for the next five years. Only after these or other life events are settled will he or she be ready and available to you. You get my point? Even if you are lucky enough to be ready in your own life, you can't control the timing of someone else's. The only thing you can do is to have faith that your love is out there somewhere, and be as ready for him or her as you can be when he or she enters your life. Follow my program and it'll help you enjoy your life in the meantime, and ensure that you're your best, most attractive self when your soul mate does appear.

My experiences with clients and others who share their stories with me inform my viewpoints, and as you'll read, my examples. But I've also found that there's nothing new under the sun. It seems that relationship and dating issues are very much the same for everyone.

In the following pages, you'll read about people who are new to the dating world and people who have decades of experience; self-made millionaires and financially struggling graduate students; people who are leaders in their communities; people who are stay-at-home moms; and countless others. You'll see that some very successful people can do some very silly things when it comes to relationships and dating, but don't be too quick to judge. I bet there are plenty of examples of clients who have made the same mistakes that you have in the past, or could potentially make in the future. My point is that we all do some goofy things in our dating and relationship lives, but hopefully this book will help you to prevent possible disasters and smooth the road to finding your soul mate.

Remember, the Lonely Hearts Club has a huge membership. You are not alone. Keep reading to learn more about my three simple steps to finding love and happiness. Your soul mate awaits!

Please send me an email at Judith@SoulMatesUnlimited.com to let me know how it goes! I hope my book helps you and I wish you love.

Judith Gottesman, M.S.W.
Marin County, California

INTRODUCTION

> *People think a soul mate is your perfect fit, and that's what everyone wants. But a true soul mate is a mirror, the person who shows you everything that is holding you back, the person who brings you to your own attention so you can change your life.*
>
> — Elizabeth Gilbert, author of *Eat, Pray, Love*

What Is a Soul Mate? Do They Really Exist? And Can You Have More Than One?

As the daughter of a rabbi, I know that Jewish theology has a definite view on soul mates. The main idea is that God picks a soul mate for each and every one of us, even before we are born. We even have a word for it: *bashert*, meaning preordained by God. The importance of it is often explained by way of the following rabbinical story:

> *During Roman times, a rich matron once asked a rabbi, "If your God created the universe in six days, what has God been doing since?"*
>
> *The rabbi replied that God had been arranging marriages, an idea the wealthy woman found laughable.*

> *"Anyone could do that!" she replied. The rabbi held his ground, saying that picking the proper spouse was as difficult as parting the Red Sea.*
>
> *The matron decided to prove the rabbi wrong by ordering 1,000 of her slaves to get married; she herself hurriedly matched them all up. The following morning, the slaves were wailing, begging to be released from their marriages, and some of them even had injuries — a black eye, a broken foot, an injured head — to prove how bad even one night with the wrong person had been.*
>
> *The woman finally had to admit that the rabbi was right: Matchmaking was best left up to God.*

So how do matchmakers, singles clubs, and dating sites fit into this divine plan? I'll get to that in Part 3: the **Act** section.

What is a soul mate?

We've all heard it before, so it may sound cliché, but I believe it is true: Your soul mate is truly your best friend and lover. He or she is the person you most want to spend time with, either in conversation or silence; the person you are physically most attracted to, and that attraction endures over time, even grows deeper with time. Your soul mate accepts you and wants the best for you, even more than he or she wants the best for him- or herself. In fact, you inspire your soul mate to be a better person. As Jack Nicholson's character finally comes to believe in the film *As Good As It Gets,* "You make me want to be a better man."

Contrary to popular opinion, soul mates don't need to be just like you or share all of your interests. What's important however, is that your soul mate shares most of your values and your outlook on the world. After all, your passion for boating may ebb and flow, but your ideas on how to make sense of this crazy world likely won't change much over time. Don't get me wrong, it's great if you share interests with your partner, but you don't have to share all of them. After all, a real spice to a relationship is someone who can expose you to new experiences, new places, and new interests. Also, many of us seek *complementary* qualities in a mate. For example, that shy guy might be attracted to that loud, vivacious gal that some bolder men might find overwhelming.

As I've mentioned, for a successful relationship it's important that you and your mate share values. And one value that's sometimes overlooked in these discussions concerns what both of you want from a relationship. It's not unheard of for someone who is looking for a spouse to change the mind of someone who thought she was simply searching for a casual relationship, but it definitely makes everything easier — and will help avoid a lot of tears — if both of you are looking for the same kind of relationship at the same time.

I believe we're here on this Earth to make the world a better place and that your soul mate helps you with that task. Your soul mate is also here to make you a better person

— a task that starts simply by believing in you. Your soul mate makes you want to be the best version of yourself, the version you probably didn't even know you had in you until you met them. Your soul mate can do this because they already see you that way, and by seeing the best possible version of you and believing it without a doubt, you slowly begin to see past your own insecurities and foibles and see yourself the way your soul mate does: perfect, just as you are. And the better you believe you are, the better you become. It is a virtuous circle.

I believe a note here on what a soul mate *isn't* is called for. While I've said that a soul mate pushes you to be a better person, this pushing should always be in a positive general direction. If "encouragement" verges into the negative, taking the form of constant belittling or putting you down in the course of your normal everyday interactions, I think it's time to take a second look at the person with whom you're involved.

This isn't to say that your soul mate will never hurt your feelings. They probably will, and some people just have a thicker skin than others. But if your partner is constantly putting you down under the guise of "helping you to become a better person," she or he probably doesn't love you unconditionally, as you are.

Although a soul mate will encourage you to be your best possible version of yourself, they will never, ever try to change your core self for them. This fact was brought home to me when one client told me that her boyfriend had recently asked her to marry him, but that he wanted her to get rid of her beloved poodle before he would move in with her. He wasn't allergic; he just didn't like dogs. Another person wanted this monogamous woman to marry him, but be in an "open marriage." Stay true to your core values and never change them for another person. Your soul mate will never ask that of you.

I unequivocally told both of them that these men weren't their soul mates. The first woman had always had dogs in her home and in her life, and she didn't think she would be happy knowing she would never live with a dog again. I knew that even if she found a good home for her poodle, her resentment toward her new husband would only grow and fester. The other boyfriend's claims that additional partners would enhance a marriage and make it and their sex life "more fun" are contrary to what she believed to be the whole point of marriage and a committed life with one special person. Core value problems like these only have a way of getting larger as a marriage goes on, so don't ignore the red flags.

Can you have more than one soul mate?

Although the biblical story I told seems to imply that God plans one and only one match for each person on Earth, I can't believe that's true. The facts simply don't support this.

I have seen too many people blessed with more than one great love in their life to dismiss these cases. For example, I've often seen young widows or widowers go on to meet someone they love just as deeply and passionately as their first husband or wife. How can we discount these cases by saying that the new love is somehow less meaningful, or that the old love was somehow less deep?

Can you miss out on your soul mate?

Absolutely, if you have a really bad attitude about love and relationships; if you have negative feelings about the singles' dating pool; if you are a recluse who's shut off from the world; or if you are shut down emotionally and your heart is afraid of getting hurt and isn't open to real love, to name just a few examples. You can absolutely miss out on your soul mate, who will simply not recognize you or be able to penetrate your fortress of negativity and the walls you built around your heart.

While I have no magic knowledge of who has gone on to meet their soul mate if they are not a client of mine, I do sometimes field calls from prospective clients who seem so emotionally shut down or suspicious that I really wonder how they will get beyond these attitudes and find the One.

For example, I recently spoke to a high-powered business woman who gave me the third degree when she called to ask about my services. Although I expect and welcome probing questions about my approach to matchmaking and my clientele, I was floored by the tenor of her questions, which were very suspicious and cynical. As she was looking for a religious Jewish man, she actually asked me how I knew that the men I would be setting her up with were both Jewish *and* religious. I didn't know what to say, finally simply replying that I knew they were religious Jews because they told me they were.

Core religious beliefs are just not something that can be tested for. In any case, how do you ever know someone is who they present themselves to be? On a certain level, it comes down to trusting that most people won't lie to you, and the intuition that you will notice that something is awry in the rare cases that they do. If you can't have a little of this trust in yourself and others, then I think that it can be very hard for you to see the possibilities for love in your life.

I once met a widow who was attractive, youthful, financially well off, and loved to travel. She told me that she was lonely and wanted to find love. I told her that I had the perfect guy for her, a handsome retired teacher who spent his copious free time traveling the world and exploring new cultures. She backpedaled. When I dug, trying to find out why she wouldn't want to meet the guy I thought was perfect for her, I found out that she didn't want to meet him because he was a former teacher. She was closed to meeting a great guy because she was caught up in finding someone who had lots of money, like the successful businessman whom she had been married to before.

At the core of much of this type of closed behavior is *fear*, fear of getting hurt, fear of getting conned, fear of getting betrayed. It could be based on something that the person has experienced in the past; it could be something witnessed in their parents' marriage or divorce. At the core, it's a protection mechanism to avoid a broken heart or perhaps a focus on superficial things like status and money. But nothing ventured, nothing gained.

Contrast these examples with another client, a rich Silicon Valley executive who was so determined to get married that he kept two symbolic alarm clocks in his bedroom, to have one for himself and one for the yet unknown spouse on the other nightstand. He ended up marrying a woman a decade his senior and they have two great kids — worth noting, because many men I meet in my business still refuse to even consider a woman who is the same age as they are, much less older.

The moral of this story is that in order to find love, you must take a chance. Faith wins out over fear every time, so you must find ways to feed your faith to starve your fear.

Remember, if you believe that your soul mate is predestined, as I do, how can you be so presumptuous as to believe that you know who God or the universe has in store for you?

PART 1

DESIRE

For one human being to love another human being: That is perhaps the most difficult task that has been given to us, the ultimate, the final problem and proof, the work for which all other work is merely preparation.

— Rainer Maria Rilke, *The Selected Poetry*

The greatest thing you'll ever learn is just to love and be loved in return.

— Eden Ahbez

You're reading this book. So obviously your primary goal is to find your soul mate, right? Not necessarily.

Our first goal is to really figure out what it is that you want. Because of societal or familial pressures, many people have bought into the idea that they need to be partnered without ever listening to their true feelings. It's time to get in touch with those feelings.

What comes to your mind when you think of having a life partner? Do you fantasize about bringing someone home to show off at family holidays? That would be lovely, wouldn't it? Your Thanksgiving fantasy may involve lots of autumn leaves and touch football with big, strapping Kennedyesque siblings in thick sweaters, but real life often involves complicated negotiations concerning whose family to spend time with (prompting both of you to fantasize about spending Christmas in the Bahamas alone), or relatives who don't particularly treat your partner with respect or kindness. It's great when your reality looks just like the Hollywood movie of your fantasies, but just remember that those kinds of holidays may be few and far between for most of us.

More realistically, is it some notion of companionship that you're after? A dog might be a better and more reliable bet than a mate, who assuredly will have a life of his or her own and won't always want to do everything you will. Is it sex? I hate to sound promiscuous, but the reality is that you don't need to buy into the whole relationship package to find a willing sexual partner, if that's what you're after. Do you like the idea of being in a dual income couple to share finances? Perhaps your time looking for a partner would be better spent figuring out how to increase your income and decrease your expenses, for example by changing careers or finding a roommate.

The good news is that both women and men are less compelled than ever to *have* to get married. Marriage is no longer an economic imperative, and most of us are encouraged from an early age to learn how to take care of ourselves. Little boys are taught to cook, and little girls are encouraged to seek careers that will sustain them with or without a mate. No longer is marriage a necessity for survival, it is a choice — and choice, by definition, is complicated and sometimes confusing.

At the same time, because we are now encouraged to learn how to do everything to take care of ourselves, including getting an education and getting our careers well established, before worrying much about finding a mate, we as a society tend to take longer before we choose to get married or settle down. By that time, we are of course more set in our ways and likes and dislikes as people. After perfecting ourselves as single, self-sustaining beings, it's sometimes hard to open up our lives to someone who is just as independent as we are.

At this point, letting a person into our lives to jangle up our little slice of perfection can be a little scary; it may be more than some people are ready to handle, no matter how much they think they want it.

Don't get too invested in being single

Be careful not to get too comfortable or invested in being alone. Joining groups and reading books on finances for singles, for example, can sometimes mentally set you up for a life alone. Instead, you want to concentrate on opening up your world so that you're inviting someone else into it, to join you in your nice life.

For example, I know one very attractive and successful woman who became a client two years ago, when she was 34; let's call her Kate. I recently gave her a call to tell her about a man who I thought would be a perfect match for her. She was clearly interested and called me back for details, but she also told me that she had recently begun dating a man who wanted to take their dating to the next level and become exclusive. She confessed that although she really liked the man, was attracted to him, and desired a serious relationship with him, she had great fun going out on dates with a variety of different men and was having a difficult time with the idea of settling down. As a fashion designer who lives in San Francisco, her life had become reminiscent of an episode of *Sex and the City*.

She had become very used to a certain lifestyle: logging on to her dating apps daily to see which men had contacted her, and whom she might like to meet up with that weekend; shopping for new going-out-on-the-town outfits; and working out at the gym to stay in shape for those little dresses.

On one hand, Kate, now 36, told me that she really desired a soul mate and wanted to have children, but on the other hand she was having a fabulous time as a single woman. In fact, she had become so used to her fabulous single lifestyle that she said she wasn't even sure how to change her life, even *if* she wanted to settle down with one guy. And, although she had signed on with me for my matchmaking services, she hadn't quite figured out if she really *desired* a life partner at this point.

I believe, of course, that whether she really desires a soul mate or not, her confident and easygoing attitude, natural sociability, friendly smile, and the absolute lack of desperation that she projects are the very qualities that make her desirable to potential mates — lessons for anyone who seeks connection with another human being.

A discussion about desire is intimately connected with the idea that involving a true partner in your life requires an amazing amount of open-heartedness and flexibility. The rewards are many, but the road to get there can be challenging for a person used to life on their own.

And you don't have to live a fabulous life like Kate to be uncomfortable with the idea of changing your situation. Another woman I know, Tessa, is a corporate lawyer in her early 40s. A little on the full-figured side, she told me that she was having a difficult time meeting men that loved her curves. Unhappy in her career, yet at the same job for more than a decade, Tessa told me that finding love and having a family of her own were her primary goals.

But when I told her that I had just the right guy for her—a pediatrician with his own practice who is attractive, owns his own home, prefers women with curves, and says that the only thing missing from his life is a family (including a dog whom he hopes his future wife will help him pick out at the shelter) — Tessa balked. The problem was that he lived an hour away by plane, and she didn't see a future with someone whose thriving medical practice precluded him from moving to her city. I gently reminded Tessa that she told me she hated her job, and that she could get a new one if she found herself in love and willing to move.

Or take Lucy. Never married and in her late 40s, she also told me that finding love and having a family were the primary goals in her life. But when I suggested a potential match in another town, Lucy replied that since she just redid her kitchen and bought new window treatments, she couldn't consider moving, even for a soul mate.

Tessa and Lucy don't seem to love singlehood the way Kate does, but they are no less unwilling to rock their worlds, even when their worlds don't have a lot that they love, beyond a safe career path and lovely interior design. The point is that, whether by encouraging you to spend a lot more nights at home, socialize with their friends as much as with your friends, and even possibly move away or change careers to be with them, your true love will shake up your life in ways that might not always be comfortable.

A soul mate will rarely fit perfectly into your life as it is. And, this fact can be truly scary if you've spent years of singlehood getting used to a certain lifestyle—be it good, bad, or a little bit of both.

True desire for a soul mate is a desire for unparalleled intimacy; it's a desire to share your fantastic life with another, to give and receive love, joy and support from them, and to always put their feelings either before your own, or at least on equal footing with yours. It's love that is unselfish at its core. And, while it may (and should!) begin with amazing sexual attraction and unbridled lust, it will grow over time into something much, much deeper.

More on the Soul Mate Effect™

This process of opening your heart to another is never easy. If it were, you'd be running around with your heart on your sleeve, vulnerable to every emotion and person that happened to waft your way. It's natural and good to want to protect yourself in life and in love, but this normal inclination toward self-protection must be balanced with a healthy openness, an appreciation for the possible in life to let your soul mate in.

Once you do, before you know it, you'll find yourself wondering how you lived prior to meeting this person. You may even notice that all aspects of your life have improved considerably, just by virtue of having someone who is there, on your side and in your corner. This is one of the telltale ways to know that you have really met your soul mate, by the way: Your entire life gets better!

Of course, in the first passionate months of a relationship, when all you can focus on is each other, a few work or school projects may slide or your finely calibrated exercise routine may go on semipermanent hiatus, but after a while you'll see that you're actually doing better at work and that you're more energetic than ever, even if you don't go to the gym quite as obsessively as before. This is the Soul Mate Effect™ in action.

By the way, we've all experienced what the Soul Mate Effect™ *isn't.* This is when a love affair leaves you feeling worse off than before — even before you break up! When you are in the wrong relationship, just as when you are in the right relationship, you may initially feel giddy and in love, but over time the relationship begins to sap you of your strength and energy, your confidence, even your sense of self. In most cases, this is not because your partner is a bad person; it's simply because this person isn't the right person for you, nothing more, nothing less.

Movin' on

This may sound obvious, but it's worth saying: As soon as you realize that overall your life is getting worse rather than better when in a love relationship, it's time to end that relationship and move on, no hard feelings. There's no point in staying in a relationship that dampens your wonderful life; this is not the right relationship for you and staying in it even a minute longer than you need to just serves to block or delay you from meeting your true love match.

This doesn't mean everything will be easy when you meet "the One." As I've said, opening your heart to let in another isn't always easy. In the early stages of your relationship there may well be bumps in the road: crying sessions, discussions about breaking up, miscommunication, and hurt feelings. We are all unique individuals with our own particular pasts, families, and ways of being. Unfortunately, we don't often recognize our own uniqueness, believing instead that our thought processes and emotional reactions are "typical."

I'm here to tell you that typical does not exist, and that it will take some time for a loving partner to understand you and you to understand them, even if you are soul mates. In fact, you may never understand every single thing about your partner, and that's OK. Different ways of looking at the world can even be a source of excitement and creativity in your relationship. What's really essential is that you believe your partner's explanations of their emotions and reasoning, and that you honor those feelings without imposing your own judgments on them. These are the kinds of relationships where, after 50 years, a husband will say about his wife, "After all this time, she still surprises me!"

For this reason, you must realize that getting out of a clearly wrong relationship is not the same thing as "cutting and running" every time the going gets tough, especially in the early stages of a relationship when you both are still figuring each other out and exploring what you want for the future.

How does all this relate to desire? I'm simply trying to get across that a desire for a soul mate cuts way beyond familial or societal obligations, fantasies about Hollywood romance, or the idea that you will find someone who is essentially your twin. Desiring a soul mate is about being willing to get to know yourself, going deep to accept another, and being interested in growing as a person. The growth part is essential, as letting someone else into your life on this level will challenge you in ways you didn't know were possible. And the rewards will manifest in ways you never could see coming.

That's why the "shopping" that you see so often today for love matches is so often doomed to failure. Although I'm not opposed to internet dating or mass-market dating services, they too often encourage us to look at dating in the wrong way. Age, financial status, body type, and the like all have their importance when seeking a match; however, none of them will add up to one if the match isn't meant to be. What is of far greater importance is chemistry, a quality that just can't be accounted for via an algorithm.

We use the checkboxes because they represent something we can measure and quantify. They represent guideposts for us, helping us to get to know ourselves while we continue looking for our match. They are the metrics for a part of life that is essentially unquantifiable and somewhat out of control. Once we meet the right person, we'll throw away our list. Our match will surely meet some of these important criteria, but he or she will also fail to measure up in innumerable ways — and it simply won't matter. After all, as Helen Keller wrote, "The best and most beautiful things in the world cannot be seen or touched. They must be felt with the heart."

To answer the question "Are you ready to let a soul mate in?" think about this: Are you ready for your life to be turned upside down — in a good way, of course?

Discover your blocks

The first step to clearing the way for your soul mate is really exploring your core beliefs, unearthing any ambivalence, and *deciding that you want to find him or her.* If you haven't been successful in the past, it's time to confront what may be holding you back, if anything.

It may be true that you are deeply committed to sharing your life with an intimate partner and simply haven't found the right person yet; however, it may be instead that you have blockages to undertaking this exciting yet potentially frightening adventure. There's nothing wrong with that. Examine these questions, and feel free to add your own:

- What do I enjoy about being single?
- What are my goals and priorities in life, and where does love fit?
- Do I believe that I might be better off alone?
- What scares me about the thought of being in a relationship? (losing control, loss of independence, being vulnerable, having to compromise, sacrificing my lifestyle, etc.)
- Am I still connected to a past relationship or person?

You may realize that you've been unconsciously stymieing your dating life because you haven't really faced up to the answers to these questions. Depending on what you discover about yourself, you may realize any number of things: that you've just been going through the motions of finding a partner because dating is fun, and you're not ready to settle down yet (an entirely acceptable and healthy conclusion, by the way); that you have more important goals than finding love right now; or that a current or past love is blocking your way, inhibiting you from moving on.

One useful exercise for answering the big questions about desire is to do a "relationship resume" of past loves to spot patterns in your behavior. Once you spot the behavioral patterns, it's a lot easier to see what may be motivating you to get involved with certain types of people, for good or bad, and to analyze that in the context of Figuring Out What You Really Want.

An effective relationship resume requires a great deal of self-reflection and total honesty, which is scary, I know. But do your best. Remember, this is not a document that requires sharing. In fact, when you're finished, I recommend that you hide your resume deep in your computer files or at the bottom of your underwear drawer; this is an exercise for your eyes only. (While you may be tempted to do so, don't burn this document in your fireplace. You'll need to look at it again for purposes I'll describe later in the book.)

To make your resume, simply grab a sheet of paper, draw three columns, and reflect on your relationship history. Include anyone who *really* mattered to you, even if the relationship lasted only two or three weeks. In the first column, list the person's name. In the second column, note *who* chose to end the relationship, you or the other person. In the final column, list *why* the relationship ended in your most diplomatic opinion.

Once all the data is in, sit back and analyze your resume. Try to spot the patterns as they relate to desire, and be honest. If *you* chose to end most of the relationships, what were the reasons you listed? As you might be realizing, it's a red flag if you notice that you ended most of the relationships, *and* that you ended them for reasons that had to do with "getting too close, too fast," or "not ready to commit to [insert person's name here]," or for reasons that just seem plain dumb once you see them in print.

But, and this is important, even if most of the breakups were your idea, it doesn't necessarily mean that you don't really desire a soul mate. Perhaps these breakups happened long ago and your recent breakups have ended for vastly different reasons. Just as a career resume should show a progression toward jobs with expanding prestige, pay, or responsibility, your relationship resume may also show a progression in the way you behave in a relationship.

I suspect that most of you will likely find that you are somewhat ambivalent about love, that even if you *mostly* are committed and ready to find a soul mate at this point in your life, that you still have a few fears and insecurities about actually falling for someone. (After all, falling is scary in any context!) I'm here to tell you that's OK. What's important in your search for love is that you are aware of and acknowledge your own mixed feelings. Once you are aware of your hidden motivations, they no longer have the power to control you.

For example, once you admit to yourself that although you want to push your own boundaries to share your life with an intimate partner, but that at the same time you are afraid of losing your independence, you can move forward with that in mind. You may find yourself gravitating toward potential partners who have extremely demanding careers or interests that you don't share, knowing that these are the people who are most likely to let you have the space you need, just as they need their space; there is nothing wrong with this. Once you're aware that you have this fear, you can also share those feelings with a potential mate as you get to know him or her. If that person is your soul mate, trust me, they will understand.

A more serious block to finding your soul mate is that of holding on to another relationship, whether it's a relationship you're still in or have been out of for some time. Widows and widowers, of course, may hold on to a relationship with their deceased partner for years, and may need specific professional help to move on, when and if they choose to.

Are you unavailable?

I find that one all too obvious yet all too common inhibition to finding your true love is being in a relationship with someone else. Indeed, it's very difficult to find your "one" when you're stuck in a time- and energy-consuming relationship — especially if that relationship is exclusive, meaning that dating other people is not an option. (Do you really think that your soul mate is going to encourage you to be a cheater? Not likely, and I wouldn't trust them if they did.) Again, I urge you to get out of the unsatisfying relationship as soon as you can after you realize that it isn't getting you anywhere.

I do realize that this is easier said than done. It takes an enormous leap of faith to go from having a relationship, even if we feel that it isn't completely right, to having no relationship at all. Many people never seem to be able to take this step. We all have friends who seem to go from relationship to relationship with no discernable break in between. It almost seems that they've lined up their next relationship, even before saying *adiós* to their future exes, and then we pretend to be surprised when their new flame doesn't work out. This isn't a healthy pattern, and it doesn't lead to finding a soul mate. These people are needy and are displaying addictive behavior; they don't much care who fills the lover role, as long as someone does.

Feeling the pain for a past failed relationship is a necessary step to healing. Allow yourself time to feel and to heal and then to move on. (Some people go from relationship to relationship and never allow themselves to feel the pain. Others seem to get stuck in the story of a failed relationship or partner, brewing negative feelings about future relationships and setting themselves up for failure.) Remember, as that old song '70s song goes, "Once you get past the pain, you'll learn to find your love again."

For most of us, getting *out* of a wrong relationship is a lot more difficult than getting *into* a wrong relationship. We all want to be wanted. Even if the wrong person isn't treating us well, it's hard to let go. If you're having trouble making a break, this may be a good time to seek help from a therapist to explore your feelings. At the very least, talk to a good friend who is clearly on your side, rather than to a mutual friend.

Sometimes, when breaking up is hard to do, it can be tempting to keep the relationship going by half measures. You may start to make deals, like agreeing to an open relationship, where you stay together but agree to allow each other to see other people. Or you may try to be "just friends," or even "friends with benefits." For most people these scenarios rarely work after being in a committed, monogamous relationship for any length of time, simply because it's too difficult. For all but the highly evolved, jealousies, negotiating, and obsessing will start to take up precious emotional energy. How will you ever find your soul mate while you're embroiled in such drama? Try to make a clean break. It may sound harsh, but you may likely even need to avoid seeing each other as friends.

This situation relates to the other way you can hold on to a relationship: when a relationship has been over for a period of time, but you are still attached to that person or to that relationship.

For example, I once met with a client and complimented her on a ring she was wearing. She replied, "Thank you; it was given to me by my soul mate." Then she proceeded to tell me all about this sexy guy she's dated for years who gave it to her, and how they still see each other when he calls, but he won't commit to her. This was a very attractive and successful woman in her early 50s who had never married.

I asked her if she wore that ring on dates, and she admitted that she did. *What's wrong with this picture?* Does she tell prospective mates who compliment her on her ring where she got it, or just me, the matchmaker? And does it really matter? Even if she doesn't talk about the man who gave her the ring, just the fact that she isn't over this man — describing him as her soul mate — means that she isn't deep-down open to anyone else at this point in time.

Another situation I see time and time again, especially in cities like San Francisco and New York where housing prices are sky-high, is the "broken up but still living together" scenario. Now how can you really cut the cord of a past relationship if you still have to see that person in the kitchen every day? I've even heard of past lovers who still share a bed because they only have one bedroom. The complications are endless and will really impede moving on with your life and meeting your Real Great Love — and forget bringing home that potential love to your apartment. My advice: *Get thee out of the apartment, posthaste!*

You may hold on to the idea that the relationship can be rekindled; you may fantasize that the person was your true love (even though the fact that the relationship ended should pretty much negate that delusion); or you may hate your former lover so strongly that you avoid entire neighborhoods to make sure you never run into him or her. Whether the preoccupations are centered on love or hate, it doesn't really matter. The truth is that you are spending your time thinking about your ex, and you are thereby impeding your openness toward the soul mate you hope to attract and invite into your life.

This scenario is also just as true for a crush. It's not necessary for you to have had a "real" relationship with someone to be obsessed by him or her. Either way, you are working against finding your soul mate when your brain space is filled with thoughts of someone who isn't going to return your love.

At the core, dealing with past relationships comes down to the central question: Are you ready for a relationship with someone new, someone who could be your soul mate?

Once you have determined that you really and truly desire a soul mate and that you no longer have any major barriers to finding one, then you are ready to take on the next step in your exciting journey: *Believe.*

PART 2

BELIEVE

Your task is not to seek for love, but merely to seek and find all the barriers within yourself that you have built against it.

— Jalal ad-Din Muhammad Rumi

I remember watching *The Wizard of Oz* on TV every single year when I was a child. I never tired of the story of Dorothy and her motley group of friends — the Scarecrow, the Cowardly Lion, and the Tin Man. They had to go through all sorts of exciting and scary adventures to get to the Emerald City, so that they could ask the Wizard to grant their wishes. Once they made it, they discovered that the Wizard couldn't help them, but through their journey Dorothy realized that they already had everything they desired: The Scarecrow had discovered that he was clever;

the Cowardly Lion had faced fear and realized he had courage; and the Tin Man had found his heart, which was there all along. But, sadly, Dorothy still wasn't home.

All seemed lost until Dorothy was given the magic mantra to make her dreams come true: Just close your eyes, tap those ruby slippers three times, and repeat "There's no place like home. There's no place like home." Once she believed with all her heart that she could go home to Kansas, she realized that she had always been there.

The Wizard of Oz might just be a children's story, but it's stood the test of time because it resonates as a classic hero's journey tale. Societies have told each other these stories for thousands of years, because they teach an important lesson about being human — basically that life is full of ups and downs, and you have to face the challenges that come your way to win what you desire. Sometimes your challenges will be against demons that are real, and sometimes they will be against demons that only exist in your own psyche, and at still other times they will be against both. Dorothy had to battle a real nemesis, but her ultimate problem was about mindset. She finally needed to believe that she could go home again.

Do you see what I'm getting at here? I believe that, like Dorothy, you may have some very real challenges to finding your soul mate, but you will also have some barriers that exist primarily in your own mind.

I'll talk more about taking concrete steps to finding your soul mate in the ***Act*** section, but this chapter is primarily devoted to 1) removing any barriers in your life toward achieving lasting love, and 2) even more importantly, working on your mindset so that you'll be emotionally prepared for love when it presents itself. After all, it's not enough to simply believe in genuine soul mate love. You also have to *believe that you deserve it.*

Lies, damned lies, and statistics

The Pew Research Center reports that the average marrying age for women is 27 and for men it's 29. But daters who are 50 and over are the fastest-growing demographic on Match.com — older people are actually the obvious demographic for online dating, since they may not have the option of meeting people at school, work, nightclubs, and bars.

> *Can you be more specific than breathing?* This is the caption on a cartoon which shows a staff person at a dating service asking this of a new client. Apparently, the client's got very low standards! You don't want to be so picky that no one measures up, but you also don't want to be so desperate that you have no standards and will settle for just about anybody. How many people focus on a resume or bank account or looks, and not how the person treats you and how you feel when you're with that person? These are the things that really matter. Remember that careers crash, money dries up, and looks fade, but real love lasts.

Every time I go online I see another article along the lines of "Best Cities for Singles" or "New Study Says Men Are Hardwired to Desire Women in Their 20s." These types of articles come from a worldview that love is something out of reach, descendants of the debunked statistic that women are more likely to die in a plane crash than to get married after 30. First, they are pop science. Two, even if they have a bit of truth, statistics don't matter — and they don't apply to the individual.

> *What's holding you back?* Most people either really don't want love due to fear of heartbreak or aren't willing to compromise to share a life with someone. So they hide away by setting up a life where there's no time for dating, whether it's because of a custody schedule (for example, kids every other day), or working all the time, or some other reason. I always find it amazing how many people are successful, confident professionals, but in their dating life they're insecure and in a constant state of confusion and anxiety.

Statistics are about lumping people together, and love is the exact opposite: Where a soul mate is concerned, you don't need to pay attention to what the mass of humanity is doing. You just need to pay attention to yourself and your own journey to find the One — and yes, all you need is one.

Thinking in terms of statistics also leads to a scarcity mentality. That is, if you are more likely to get hit by lightning than find a soul mate, for example, then you better go out on every date you possibly can so you don't accidentally miss out on him or her.

As a matchmaker, when I speak to a prospective client, I am most commonly asked what I like to call the "how many" questions. For example: *How many women do you have in my age range who have PhDs? How many men do you have who are over 6 feet tall? How many women do you have who play golf? How many men or how many women do you have in this age range? In this geographic location?* Those kinds of questions. The answer I give, no matter what specific thing they are asking about, is always the same. *It's not about the numbers.* It really and truly isn't.

I tell these would-be clients, "Say you are looking for a job. You don't want to go on 40 different job interviews, right? That would be exhausting, demoralizing, and a huge waste of time. All you need to do is go on the *right* interview." But at the same time, you don't want to make your job search so incredibly specific that you feel you can only apply for one job in a million. Same with dating. Within reason be specific, but *stay flexible.*

Just as you wouldn't want to go on an interview for every job that's posted and also wouldn't want to go on just one job interview a year, I recommend that my clients don't go on a date every day, or only once or twice a year either. Contrary to dating sites that encourage you to "swipe right" for everyone who's attractive and fulfills your bare minimum requirements, I'm asking you to 1) be more selective rather than less, and 2) accept the possibility that your soul mate might not be what you pictured, in both looks and your "List"— so you must allow sufficient flexibility to allow for variations. Remember what I said earlier, "When you find your soul mate, you'll throw away your List"? No one will be able to check all of the boxes that many of us set up, but the wonderful, surprising thing is that your true soul mate will fulfill expectations that you didn't even know you had.

You get the idea. My point is that finding a life partner isn't about the numbers, so you don't need to worry about how many dates you're getting or going out with as many people as possible. *However, you do need to believe that no matter who you are, there is someone out there for you.* And, that means that you do have to get out there in some way — whether it's via online dating (not my favorite), going to social groups and meetups, participating in religious activities or clubs, or even engaging the help of a matchmaker like me. Your soul mate isn't going to mysteriously show up at your door via UPS.

Many single people out there, but how many for you?

As you know, there are millions of people on all the dating apps. If you look at who's out there, there's no shortage of single people, likely thousands within 50 miles of where you live. How many of you have gone to a big singles event, maybe two or three hundred people at a big dance or benefit, whatever it is, and you leave alone because there isn't one person you're interested in there? But maybe then you go to a friend's dinner party and it's a small gathering, and there's only a handful of people who might be appropriate for you, and you meet this great woman or man, because it's about fate, it's about luck, it's about common values, and it's about timing. And, it's most certainly not about the numbers.

So far, everyone who's gotten married through me has married the very first person I wanted them to meet. And, I know that may change at some point, but I'm really not trying to set my clients up with a bunch of different people. How on Earth can you present your best self out there on a date if you are emotionally exhausted from dating?

Do your inner work, and figure out how to change your outer circumstances

Doing your "inner work" simply means working on your mindset so you can do what you need to do to attract your soul mate—I like to call this attraction you put out into the world the Soul Mate Effect™.

If you need to change something real in your life to be open to a soul mate, then this is where you need to concentrate your efforts. With that relationship resume in hand, ask for support from friends, read self-help books, practice mindfulness meditation, seek the services of a trusted therapist, or do whatever else feels right to you to determine what's blocking you from a soul mate relationship and how to minimize that. You may simply have the vague feeling that something in your life "isn't right." It may take time to figure out exactly what your imbalance is, so be patient and kind with yourself.

Once you figure out what your barrier or barriers are, then gather support around you to tackle those challenges. The same techniques that helped you discover the barriers in the first place may also be able to help you confront those challenges, but not necessarily. Let the nature of your challenge drive the support system you seek to confront it.

For example, if you come to the conclusion that you are geographically challenged to finding a soul mate, your support system for that will be quite different from realizing you are in a wrong relationship. Say you've determined that you're really looking for a nice Midwestern-type gal or guy, like the ones in your high school days, but you live in New York City and spend most of your dating life hanging out at nightclubs. It sounds to me like your dating technique isn't matching up with your goals. I would suggest that you change your mindset from "The best way to meet single people is to go clubbing" to "Maybe I'd meet fewer people, but more of the right type if I changed my habits." Once you do that, it's time to strategize about possible solutions — which could range in this case from the quite conservative to the very radical.

On the conservative end, if you really wanted to stay in New York City for professional or other reasons, you could join some social groups geared toward urban transplants from the Midwest. Alternatively, you could start spending more time outside of the city center and plan some activities out of town — for example, join a hiking club based in a nearby county. These types of changes don't require much support, perhaps a willing friend to join you if you need a bit of moral support to get started. (Caution: Don't use having a buddy as an excuse to avoid mingling! It's best to ask a fairly uninterested friend to attend the first session or two with you, and then tell them they're free to buzz off. You don't want potential dates to get the idea that you're more interested in or possibly romantically involved with your friend.)

On the more radical side of things, maybe you live in a small town and you've come to the conclusion that you need to move. If that's really and truly your conclusion, get started setting yourself up to do it, both mentally and practically speaking. Ask yourself, where would I like to live, and what do I need to do to make that a reality?

I can't tell you how many times I've heard from singles that there are no eligible prospects where they live. So, I say, what are you going to do about it? My question often takes people aback, because their friends, coworkers, and others don't usually suggest they move, for obvious reasons. My point is that if you've identified a problem and don't take measures to deal with that problem, then you are simply *complaining.* Is complaining going to help you to meet your soul mate? Not likely; it's likely to even turn a potential soul mate off. *But belief paired with practical action will help you meet that mate.*

Now I don't mean to minimize the life-altering impact of moving. Moving, whether it's to a nearby city or across the country, is one of the most disruptive things that you can do in life. But if your goal is really to find your soul mate and you live in a place where you already know almost every eligible person, you may really need to change your location. Otherwise, you'll be spending the rest of your days waiting for your fair maiden to gallop into town on a white horse. And as I hope you understand by now, believing that you'll find your soul mate isn't the same as magical thinking.

And, remember, just because you've realized that you probably live in a place where you won't meet your soul mate, it doesn't mean you have to take on moving all at once. Some people start going on long-distance dates, figuring that if they meet the One, then location will work itself out when one or the other decides to move. In fact, in my matchmaking, I encourage anyone who is open to moving to consider dating someone outside of their town or city to expand their pool of possibilities. Going outside your usual stomping grounds is often just the kind of shakeup you need to invite lasting love into your life.

Are you stuck in the wrong relationship?

Another barrier that could exist both in reality and in your mind is this: You may be living with or dating someone you know is wrong for you. That is a very real barrier to finding true love, isn't it?

In this example then, you must remove the barrier to finding true love by getting yourself out of that wrong relationship. Then you will be able to work on the mental barriers to finding your soul mate. But as you've probably already figured out, this kind of situation presents a catch-22: In order to remove the physical barrier, you will have to get your mindset ready. **Thus, you need to work on your mindset to take concrete steps to change your reality, but even once you've taken those first steps you must keep working on your mindset in order to take even greater steps to achieve success.**

How do you know you're stuck in the wrong relationship?

Do you fantasize about getting out of the relationship? Furthermore, do you find yourself thinking one or more of the following things when you consider leaving the relationship?

S/he is the only one who would put up with me.
No one else would love me the way s/he does.
I can't do any better than her/him.

It may take months or even years of work to get beyond these types of daunting thoughts and actually remove yourself from the wrong relationship. But if you really want to, you will do it — eventually. Unfortunately, however, your work isn't over. You will have achieved a difficult goal, but it's only one step on the way to your ultimate goal of finding your one true love. If you were Dorothy, this would be the point where you've made it to the Emerald City, but you still haven't figured out how to get home.

At this point, your mental barriers won't be focused on your old partner. So they'll sound a little different:

Maybe there just isn't anyone out there for me.
I'm probably too old at this point to find love.
All the good men/women are taken.
I need to lose another 20 pounds before anyone would even look at me.
I don't have the time to date right now.
I'm damaged goods.
Prospects for a divorced woman with three kids aren't very good.

Notice the difference? Your mindset has likely shifted at this point from focusing on your past relationship (since it's in the *past,* isn't it?) to yourself. This is potentially quite frightening, but it can also be quite liberating. After all, if your biggest barriers essentially come down to the way you feel about yourself, then you have all the power in the world to surmount them.

Getting out of a wrong relationship, of course, is just one example, and not every real barrier to finding your true love is so obvious or dire. Examples of other barriers that we may not recognize at first include: being a workaholic (when there are no prospects of meeting an appropriate mate at your office) or spending all of your free time with coupled friends (when those friends never introduce you to anyone single).

My point is simply that you must foster an awareness of how—or how not, as the case may be—your inner and outer life is set up to foster real love. Working on the mental barriers and physically real barriers to finding a soul mate is a constant process, and doing this work is part and parcel to getting what you desire.

A place called hope

A few years ago, I met a woman who became a client. To many people, it might not seem like she was the best matchmaking client: she was in her mid 60s and had never been married. Worst of all, she lived in rural Washington state. But I knew that she was a successful, attractive, intelligent, calm, kind — and most of all, *hopeful* — woman and that it was worth helping her find a match. I didn't have the right guy for her right away; it actually took two years before I set her up on her first date. But it was worth the wait.

I set Sabrina up with Larry, a divorced man about the same age who lived a couple of hours away, and who despite one bad marriage still believed in love and was very positive in his outlook. Like Sabrina, he also had a very rich life on his own and was interested in current events and culture. On their first date they went to a museum and out for coffee afterward, and they couldn't stop talking to each other. It was a match made in heaven, and they are now happily married in Seattle.

In contrast, I have met many people who are closer in attitude to Janice, a never-married woman in her early 40s who regularly does internet searches on men before upcoming dates to see if they're lying about things like marital status, profession, education level, or age. She has met a number of men through me, but no one seems good enough. There was Dave — a few inches too short, and his burgeoning tummy combined with a penchant for cheesesteaks turned her off. There was Tony — he had been divorced, so Janice figured he couldn't sustain a relationship. And, then there was Marcus; since he was a lawyer, she labeled him too confrontational. For their part, when I asked for feedback on their dates, each of these men told me that they thought Janice came off as angry and judgmental, and no wonder!

Now it could be that none of these men were good matches for Janice, but based on her negative, suspicious, hypercritical feedback about each and every one, and their feedback about her, I suspect that Janice feels that all the good guys are taken — so she is looking for red flags to prove her thesis. I completely sympathize with Janice; after years of dating without finding the One, it's hard not to have baggage. Still, is what Janice doing ultimately helping her quest to find a soul mate? Of course not.

Somehow, even though Sabrina was at least 20 years older than Janice, she had managed to keep alive her hope in finding her soul mate. Was she just naturally a more trusting, open-hearted, and resilient person? Perhaps — but probably not without a lot of conscious effort. Just as you can become more cynical and untrusting as you go through life, so you can train yourself to be more open and hopeful.

If you're bitter, jaded, and cynical about relationships and dating, terrified of getting your heart broken again, or depressed at the idea of getting back out there in the dating world, it's worth taking a few weeks or months to reprogram your mind so you have a positive attitude. (In truth, nurturing positivity is really a lifetime effort, but you can begin reconfiguring your mindset in just a few weeks.) And having a positive outlook is helpful in all areas of your life. Again, this is the Soul Mate Effect™ at work.

If you can afford it and have time, I even recommend that you take a relaxing vacation. You see, I've noticed that being in traveler mode naturally promotes an open-hearted way of seeing the world. Have you ever noticed that when traveling you tend to meet and quickly form close relationships, platonic and sometimes otherwise, with people who are different from those you normally would? This can be just the prescription for getting out of a rut and opening up your point of view on the world. And, if you're lucky, you'll be able to bring a little of that open-heartedness and joy in discovering the world back to your regular life and routine.

If reading this book isn't enough to shift your thinking, read books like *Journey of the Heart: The Path of Conscious Love* by John Welwood or *Getting the Love You Want* by Harville Hendrix, and consider seeing a therapist on a short-term basis. Do your inner work before you throw yourself into the deep end of the dating pool, so that you start off fresh and optimistic, excited about the possibilities ahead of you and the love that awaits.

And *continue* to do that inner work. Going to singles events, going on dates, doing internet dating, and just remaining open to the possibility of love can all be demoralizing, so you have to be in your best frame of mind when going through this process.

Getting out of the frantic phase

Can you get married when you've just realized that you're nearing the end of your fertility and desperate to have children? Sure, you may very well find some nice stable guy who is perfect daddy material. But will you find your soul mate while you're in this mental state? It's highly unlikely. Relationships and marriages made from this kind of mutual "it's time to meet My One True Love" ticking clock rarely work out over the long haul.

And, there's no doubt that there's something primitive programmed into our DNA that tells us to run the other way when we're faced with even a whiff of desperation This is yet another reason to take care of yourself both mentally and physically — aside from the obvious benefits to our well-being, it promotes the Soul Mate Effect™.

It's much easier to project strength and confidence if you really are strong, healthy, and resilient from the inside out. If you aren't already doing so, exercise, eat healthy, and get a full night's sleep as often as possible. You'll look better, have more energy, feel better about yourself, and be more confident. Make a commitment to taking care of yourself. If you're divorced with kids, a single parent, caring for aging parents, or working a 60-hour work week, I know doing these things can be difficult. It seems your kids or your boss or maybe even your ex-spouse always needs something from you. But if you're serious about finding love, it's crucial to finally make yourself the priority — and the time is now!

The time is *now* (and don't use your kids as an excuse)

I can't emphasize my point about *now* enough. I recently met a man in his 50s who got divorced when his daughters were 4 and 6. Completely devoted to his little girls, he spent all his free time with them. When they went away to college, he finally felt able to leap back into the dating pool, juggling one girlfriend in Memphis with another in Austin. After so many years of functioning only as a business owner, father, and provider, at last he was enjoying himself as a man with relationship wants and needs, and having the time of his life!

Unfortunately, this man was only able to enjoy his carefree dating life for about a year before he suffered a massive stroke and landed in a rehab hospital. He's now focused completely on his own recovery, and doesn't think he'll ever be physically or emotionally ready to have a relationship again. Attached to his image of himself as a self-sufficient and virile man, in his current debilitated state, he has lost his *belief* in finding anyone who would love him. I still hold out hope that with a little time, he'll realize he still has a lot to offer and can find love if he chooses.

Another example is a woman in her early 60s whom I interviewed. Like the man who had the stroke, she had wanted to wait until her son was out of the house and on his own before jumping back into the dating pool. She told me that her reason was that she didn't want to be like her ex-husband, who dated like crazy for a couple of years and then married a woman who didn't like children. Because of this sad situation, she vowed to give her boy everything he wasn't getting from his father, attention-love-wise.

When we met, she had been looking for love online for a couple of years and was upset because of the difficult time she was having with internet dating; she specifically found that many men her age were looking for younger women (unfortunately not an unusual situation). I wondered to myself why she thought she had to "sacrifice" all those prime years of her life for her son, when so many people with children are able to date and marry new spouses who are crazy about kids. If she hadn't been so caught up in the martyr role, perhaps she would've found a wonderful, loving man who would've been the loving father figure to her son that her ex-husband, distracted by a new wife and new life, no longer was. She still had plenty of opportunity to meet her soul mate, but because it wasn't as easy as it was in the fantasies she had spun for herself during those lonely years, she was feeling beaten down and hopeless.

Both of these people said that they wanted to find someone, but they didn't truly make themselves a priority in their own lives. Just when they had planned to get serious about their own happiness, unforeseen circumstances caused their beliefs to become focused on the impossibility — rather than the hope — of finding love.

To me, the saddest part of these stories is the fact that both of these people put their own happiness aside to "focus" on their children. Children, first and foremost, need happy, loving, authentic parents to model their own future selves upon. Do we really want to teach our children that when they grow up, their own happiness won't matter? Children thrive when parents are happy, loving, and affectionate with them — qualities that are hard to fake when we are not really and truly happy. And no child wants to be the constant object of parental focus, no matter how loving!

Furthermore, children are so perceptive and wise; I think it would be extremely difficult to tell yourself that you are sacrificing looking for a mate "for the sake of the children" and not have your children pick up on this attitude. Every time you seem lonely or sad, your children, who love you limitlessly, will think that it's their fault for keeping you from your happiness. If, like the folks I just mentioned, you then look for a mate in your later years, and God forbid, *don't* find him or her, how do you think your children will feel then?

I'm certainly not advocating that you date thoughtlessly when you have children. You need to be careful who you let into your children's lives, and how quickly, and make sure that they will love, cherish, and protect your children just as you would. But becoming a martyr mother or father is not the answer, and could very well lead to bitterness on your part and guilt in your children.

Of course, kids aren't the only excuse people give for delaying their own happiness — work and school are also tops on the list — but I believe that the children issue merits particular thought, because it involves people other than you. After all, if you work too much and never find your soul mate, your decision affects only you (and perhaps your soul mate out there looking for you). But if you use your children as an excuse to delay your happiness, your decision directly affects them, their outlook on life, and even *their* happiness. Your attitude can actually have negative effects from generation to generation.

Think about it: First, consider your happiness as a parent. I firmly believe that one of the number one things you can do to assure happiness in both the present and in the future for your sons or daughters is to model being a happy adult. After all, what effect do you think it has on children to grow up with parental martyrs who blame their lack of happy, loving, romantic relationships on their children?

In the present, the message passed on to your kids is a mixed one that goes something like this:

1) Having children ruined my life.
2) You *are* my life (an attitude especially detrimental to boys when taken by mothers).
3) Ensuring the happiness of others is more important than my own happiness (an attitude especially detrimental to girls, no matter which parent espouses it).
4) My worth is tied up in you, my child, and how well you do in life — so you better not disappoint me since I've sacrificed so much for you.
5) Because of my sacrifice, I OWN YOU.

Now this says nothing of parents that are *happily* single. Parents don't need to be partnered to be great parents. I'm simply speaking of the parents who decide that, for fear of somehow harming their children or taking their eye off the ball of child-rearing, that they can delay their own happiness, even though they'd love nothing more than finding another adult to love and cherish in a soul mate relationship.

Even if your children can somehow use their teens and young adulthood to make it through this minefield of negative feelings about the parent-child relationship, if you have a negative attitude about romantic relationships in general, this too can be passed on.

In my experience as a matchmaker, I've actually noticed what seems to be an epidemic of young and middle-age people thinking that healthy, loving marriages are a fantasy, since they never saw anything of the sort as they grew up. These people can't seem to settle down or commit, and may miss out on happy coupledoms, since they don't believe in the institution of marriage or even long-term, lasting relationships. These are the people who spend their lives swiping on dating sites and going on countless coffee dates that never seem to lead anywhere more than a hookup. Speaking of hookups …

Bringing sexy back — and friends with benefits

In this chapter, I've talked about the idea that you need to prepare yourself from the inside out to be ready to invite love into your life. I've talked about the need to prepare yourself mentally for love by clearing past relationships; stowing your relationship baggage; being open to love in places you might not expect (such as in a different city), or with a person you did not expect; and remembering that there is no time like the present to want the best for yourself.

I've mentioned mindfulness meditation, self-help books, and therapy as particular techniques to help shake us out of past patterns and put us into a mind frame for Belief in love. Now, I'd like to turn my attention to another technique that I've seen, on an unscientific basis, work again and again: getting sexy. Perhaps we should call it the Sex Effect™.

How do you start feeling sexy? By acting sexy! Dusting off your flirting techniques, buying some new clothes that make you feel attractive, and getting a makeover or new haircut will all help make you feel sexier (more on these peacock displays of sexiness in the **Act** section). But perhaps the best way to get that sexy glow is to actually *have sex!*

'Sex Buddy' Benefits

- It's a great cardio workout.
- It's a great workout for certain muscles.
- You aren't desperate to be in a relationship with just anyone to be having sex.
- You feel sexy when you have an active and satisfying sex life. In other words, you are benefiting from the Sex Effect™.
- You're more attractive to others when you are having sex, and more relaxed and confident. No matter your age, the hormones and pheromones flow and your skin glows when you're sexually active and fulfilled.

We've all noticed it. When we're sexually active, people just seem drawn to us (even if we do look a little rumpled and our hair is a little messy). Why is this? Research suggests that sexual intercourse can reduce pain, decrease stress, and boost immunity — all attractive attributes. In fact, one researcher, Dr. David Weeks, formerly head of old-age psychology at the Royal Edinburgh Hospital, recently performed a study reporting that regular sex can make both men and women look five to seven years younger!

Intercourse causes the release of human growth hormone (which makes skin look more elastic); estrogen (which imparts that dewy glow); oxytocin and endorphins (which promote relaxation and healing); and literally helps us sweat out toxins and sleep better. It's no wonder this chemical bath makes us look better and smile more, and the confidence we then project to the outside world results in a virtuous circle of more smiling, flirting, and increased confidence. We're more desirable when we're in love!

But you don't have to be in love to use sexual chemistry to your advantage. If you're open to the idea, sex with a trusted friend can confer many of the same benefits as sex with an intimate partner; either way, call it greasing the wheels for the Sex Effect™. And sex with a good buddy undoubtedly offers more benefits than sex with a partner in a going-nowhere or less-than-happy relationship.

I know this may be a controversial idea for many who feel sex has to be a part of a loving, committed relationship, and I would never suggest that anyone do anything that he or she isn't comfortable with, but if you *are* comfortable with the idea, consider it. Unless you're asexual or very religious, long-term celibacy isn't realistic for most single people, and I believe that it's better to have sex with a friend you love and trust than to rush into sex with someone you're not absolutely sure about just because you're craving a physical bond.

The latter often leads to an "accidental relationship" with a person you were never really interested in to begin with, which then cuts off the opportunity for you to find your true love — at least until you finally manage to extricate yourself from the accidental relationship. Along the way, both you and your "accident" have no doubt aged emotionally, if not physically, and countless tears have been shed.

The key to having a "friend with benefits" and harnessing the power of the Sex Effect™ is 1) to choose that friend very wisely, and 2) for both parties to communicate, communicate, communicate. Remember that this relationship is no less important than a soul mate relationship, and you need to make sure that everyone's needs are being met. You need to make sure you're not leading anyone on, and that your friend understands what you want out of this arrangement, and is really and truly OK with it. After all, a good friend relationship may very well outlast a marriage. You don't want to ruin something special.

Of course, no matter who you have sex with, all of the same rules of the game apply. Always play it safe and be sure to use a condom to avoid sexually transmitted infections or getting pregnant.

Benefits notwithstanding, a sex buddy relationship simply won't work out for everyone, whether it's because there's no suitable partner around, moral or religious reasons, or other issues. In these cases, don't forget sex for one. If you can't find someone you trust to be your sex buddy or just aren't comfortable with the idea, you can always take care of business, so to speak, on your own. If you need help learning more about this, check out the classic *Sex for One: The Joy of Selfloving* by Betty Dodson.

Rejection? What's that?

You may have the desire, but without a strong, confident belief that 1) you deserve love and 2) your soul mate is out there, it will be hard to sustain the momentum necessary to act.

Somehow, you have to be mentally ready for "rejection." It's tough to not be picked or pursued, but the other person is actually doing you a favor. Anyone who rejects you wasn't for you anyway. One male client of mine told me he was on a dating site, and that about 100 women a day viewed him but didn't contact him. It felt like a personal rejection. But even though it feels really personal when things like this happen, it's not. It's a gift.

You can also extend this way of thinking to dates or relationships you've already had. Realize that there's no such thing as rejection. If it doesn't work out, that person was simply not for you, no big deal. Whether it's a first date that never turned into a second or an internet profile that didn't get replies, it's not rejection. These dismissals are just putting you one person closer to meeting your soul mate. There is also the idea that a date or relationship that didn't work out was meant to be, that the person had something to teach you.

Do you like yourself and your life? If you can't answer yes to both of these questions, why would anyone want to share your life with you?

The most important qualities in finding love, by far, are the belief that your love is somewhere out there and the ability to stay hopeful that your love will find you.

Believe there is someone out there for you. People who don't give up, believe they'll find love, and stay open increase their chances for a soul mate relationship. Having hope is the primary ingredient for taking action. So the key, then, is to *be hopeful* and *be able to sustain that hope* over the long term, despite bad dates or relationships that veer south.

When my clients tell me they feel lonely and discouraged, I sometimes try to remind them of that verse from "Lonely People" by 1970s band America:

This is for all the single people
Thinking that love has left them dry
Don't give up until you drink from the silver cup
You never know until you try.

A final word on Belief

Try to feel as good as you can when you have a bad date or end a relationship you're not into. It means you're freed up from wasting time on the wrong person and one person closer to the right one. Your love will find you as long as you shine your unique light: Be your authentic self.

Are you not sure who that is anymore? I guarantee you knew who it was when you were a child, before becoming weighed down by life and damaged by past relationships. Do the work to figure out who you are *now* — at this particular stage in your life. Does it jibe with who you were when you were young? Is it authentic? Reassess what you want and who you want.

PART 3

ACT

You can't stay in your corner of the Forest waiting for others to come to you. You have to go to them sometimes.

— *Pooh's Little Instruction Book,*
written by Joan Powers,
inspired by the books of A. A. Milne

I'm often asked: "Isn't love really about fate? Does a person really need to try this hard, put in this much effort to find love? Won't he or she just find me, won't I just stumble upon him or her at the grocery store, or in the class I'm taking, or just somehow walking down the street? Couldn't I simply hang out at home and wait?" After all, at some point the TV will go on the fritz, or maybe a fender bender will happen in the front yard. God will just send out a cable repair person or a cop — who will, of course, be that special someone you've been waiting for.

In other words: *if your match is preordained, why are you spending all of this time and energy on internet dating, singles clubs, and yes, even matchmakers?*

I get it; it is tiresome. And you know what? It *is* about fate, but that doesn't mean you don't have to be proactive. Your soul mate is not going to just come knocking at your door while you sit home reading a book or watching TV. You really have to make some sort of an effort. Whether you believe in God, or the universe, or whatever, I think people — when they actually make a concerted effort, and they open their hearts and minds to finding love, and say, "I'm finally ready to be happy and have love in my life, and share my life with someone" — the vast majority of people will find it. It's truly amazing!

So much of the time, once you just change your mindset and you put it out there and you have a light in your eyes and a smile on your face and an openness in your heart, that's when you will find your love. It's really a miracle. But it's not a miracle without effort. And that's why people hire me; that's why I encourage people to go to events, and do all those other things to try to meet people, because you just never know when and where and how you're going to meet your match — and you want to be open and ready when she or he comes along.

So, if you've ever fantasized that your love interest would ride in on a white horse and love you forever, please recognize this idea for the fantasy that it is. That's why Jewish tradition has another concept to teach us: It's not enough to just have a *bashert*. In other words, you have to get off your tush to find your *bashert*.

I'm going to bring up *The Wizard of Oz* again here. Dorothy started off her journey a little whiny, remember? "I want to go home. I want to go home!" And that attitude didn't get her very far with Glenda the Good Witch, who pointed her toward a long march straight down the yellow brick road. Only after Dorothy's marathon trek, dodging the Wicked Witch of the West, evil trees, sleep-inducing poppies, and winged monkeys, did Glenda share with her the secret of getting back to Kansas.

I find that most things in life, including finding a soul mate, work pretty much like these types of classic hero's journey tales. As we all try to teach our kids, we appreciate everything so much more when we work for the things we want. It's just human nature not to value what comes too easily to us. I think personally that's why so many of us wistfully look back at "what might have been" relationships and jobs that came too easily to us in our younger years, and which we didn't properly value, protect, and nurture.

You have to believe that soul mates exist and you have to believe that you deserve love. How many people sabotage their chance at happiness? You think it's not the right time;

you're busy in your career; you're still in graduate school; you haven't been divorced that long. How many chances do you think you get at happiness? Make the most of it when someone wonderful comes your way, even if the timing and package aren't what you planned. Who said your soul mate had to have everything on your List or the perfect resume? Maybe the person who's perfect for you is completely different than you ever imagined and your life will be full of wonderful surprises, bigger and fuller than you ever could have conceived.

All of this is to say: If you want a meaningful relationship, you're going to have to work for it!

So you've gone through the first two steps to make sure you're in the right space to embark on your quest for a soul mate. You both ***Desire*** a partner and you really, really ***Believe*** that your perfect person is out there for real. The third and final step is to simply get up off your tush and make it happen.

But how? Let's start with teaching you how to flirt.

How to catch their eye and keep 'em looking

First, a few flirting *don'ts:*

Don't get overly touchy. Of course, a little is fine — and even good — but there's a fine line between flirting and sexual harassment. You don't want to invade someone's personal space. When approaching a person, stay a comfortable distance from their face and don't touch their body in an inappropriate manner. It can freak them out, or at the very least, turn them off. Along with this comes understanding when to take no for an answer. It's important to hear them loud and clear, and not dismiss their response if they aren't reacting positively. Don't take it personally.

Don't force yourself to go out if you're in a bad mood, unless you're the type of person who knows that getting out will make you feel better. While you might feel like you need to go out as much as possible to try to meet someone, there's no point if you're not mentally up to it. Now, you might say, "I'm never up to it." And I would understand, because it's not easy putting yourself out there, especially after a long day at the office.

Transitioning from work to play doesn't come naturally to everyone. If you're burnt out and really just want to go home and watch Netflix (as opposed to "Netflix and chill" with a romantic buddy), do it. Just don't give into this impulse all the time, because you might never go out. Remember, meeting your soul mate isn't a numbers game and you're unlikely to meet your match if you're not putting your best self forward. Unless, of course, your dream is meeting a fellow misanthrope.

Skip the crowd. Who you are with makes a big difference in how approachable you are. When you go out, don't surround yourself with too many friends, especially those of the opposite gender, or your subject of interest might be intimidated to make the first move. On that note, don't go to a place that's too crowded, you won't stand out.

You go first. Sometimes no matter how hard you try, it's hard to get somebody to approach you. When all else fails, make the first move. It's okay, and the other person might be really flattered by the attention. After all, what's the worst they can do?

Don't act distracted … by the basketball game playing on the bar's widescreen or the impulse to get another beer, and, for goodness' sake, don't look around for other prospects while you're talking to someone. She or he *will notice.* The kiss of death for a potential love interest is for them to catch your wandering eye. You've flirted your heart out and connected with someone, don't blow it by overtly checking out others around the room. Focus on talking to the person in front of you, as opposed to wondering who else is there. The grass is rarely greener on the other side.

Don't go searching for a pen or piece of paper if you meet someone. One of the best ways to lose an opportunity to get someone's number or give out yours is to be ill-prepared.

Flirting *do's* …

When you're checking someone out across the room, make direct eye contact. The key to flirting is to look someone in the eye, look away, and then look back at them, so that they know for sure you're looking at them. *Don't stare!* They'll think you're a serial killer. Just catch their eye quickly in a friendly way. Then exhibit open body language. Smile.

Have a prop. Examples of props could be interesting clothing or accessories. No, not your beer bong hat! Wear something that invites others to approach you and comment on your look: a sweatshirt with your alma mater, your favorite band, a funny (but not offensive) saying.

Laugh, it's attractive. And contagious. If you're out with friends, don't be afraid to show you're having a good time. If you come across as a fun-loving person, that will suggest you're someone who likes to enjoy themselves, appreciates friends, and welcomes the opportunity for a good laugh. You know how to let your hair down and sharing that zest for life is something you'd love to do with the right person.

Again, look into their eyes like there's no one and nothing else in the room — like time has stopped for you.

Be a good listener. Ask questions. In fact, listen more than you talk. No one likes a loudmouth, especially other big talkers. And the truth is, most people are delighted to talk about themselves. With a little prodding, people won't even notice that you haven't said a word — not that I advise you to stay completely silent during their monologue. Pretend you're a journalist and keep asking questions to keep them going! You might learn something about them, and this back-and-forth will quickly create a sense of intimacy that a more self-centered person might waste months creating.

Pay attention to your body language. If you're fidgety, it may help to hold something, buy a drink or hold a glass of sparkling water with lime (it will look like a stiff drink) and keep it in your hand. Remember that if you decide to cross your arms you're closing yourself off. When you're talking to someone, lean in. It shows you're not afraid to get close. Don't get too close though, unless you're just looking for a fling and want to get all touchy-feely.

Pay them a compliment, make them laugh, or (again) ask a question. Don't overdo it. The goal is not to embarrass someone, but to make them feel good about themselves. To make someone laugh, you definitely don't want to say anything that could be construed as offensive — remember that humor can be very subjective. So no dirty joke-telling until you know it's their style. Take it from me, asking a question is the most neutral and natural way to go, as long as you don't get overly personal right away. If you're in a gym, for example, you can ask how to use a particular weight machine. It is flattering to be asked to share your knowledge, and this can be the equivalent of paying a compliment, because the other person will feel that you consider them worthy of offering instruction.

Add your personal number to their phone. (This looks serious and less braggy than giving out your business card, like you're at a work convention.) Always volunteer your info first. If you ask for their info, they might give you a fake number if they're not sure about you yet, or they may feel like their privacy is being invaded.

If they offer their email address to you, politely ask that they give you a phone number instead. Make sure to mention that you wouldn't want your note to get lost in a pile of email.

If you get those digits, move quickly to get that date! Use the phone only to arrange it. Try not to talk for hours on end before you've had a date. You might think that a long chit-chat session is indicative of a heartfelt connection, but that's not necessarily true. It might just be that they don't know how to get off the phone with you, Chatty Cathy! For this reason, plus the danger of oversharing, you need to be aware of the subtle clues: "I really have a lot of work tonight." "I have to get up early tomorrow." And similar statements. It will show that you're aware of the other person's situation and feelings — another very attractive quality in a potential mate.

Date by numbers

Remember painting by numbers from childhood? Take a good look at yourself in the mirror. Now do it naked. How attractive are you? I have to be blunt here: You shouldn't try to date way beyond your physical range, but you should try to use your body language, humor, and other qualities to weigh the scale in your favor.

I think of a song featured in the movie *My Best Friend's Wedding*. It sounded so true to me I had to look it up. It's called "If You Wanna Be Happy" by Jimmy Soul, who sings, "If you wanna be happy for the rest of life, never make a pretty woman your wife."

I recently had to break someone's heart by telling him that my other client didn't want to see him again. It was a sad situation, but the truth was that he was basically a 7 in the looks category, but he was insisting on a 10. She was the first woman I set him up with that he liked, and it was pretty sad.

The point here is that there will be a power dynamic problem, insecurity, jealousy, etcetera, if there's a big difference between you and your mate's basic beauty.

More than a few words about internet dating

There are many ways to get a date. Some of you are very experienced at app dating, and I coach my clients on how to put your best self out there — whether online or IRL ("in real life"). Whether it's on the date itself or for your online profile, you want to present yourself in the best possible light.

Dating can be difficult and a lot of work and effort — and not just for the daters! Since I do personalized matchmaking, I'm meeting people individually, screening them, doing an in-depth interview for about an hour, and then personalizing everything, tailoring any potential matches to both individual criteria and to my own intuition. This takes into account such immeasurable qualities as the sound of their voice and the look in their eyes as well as what I consider the most important factors in making a successful match: the sharing of the same values, lifestyles, and goals.

After our initial consultation, you may not hear from me for many months; I won't contact you until I really think I have a good chance of setting you up with your match. (Incidentally, my silence has gotten me into all kinds of trouble with clients who expect me to find their match on a quick timeline. I've been on the receiving end of more angry phone calls and nasty emails than I can count. I always reply that I can't conjure a soul mate out of thin air!) I will then offer date-coaching, before or after your dates, to learn how close I was to a match and give pointers for a successful meetup.

My method is the absolute opposite of internet dating, where it's a numbers game and you're dealing with anonymous people, and you don't know whether their profiles are pumped up or just outright works of fiction. Yes, as a matchmaker, I'm definitely biased in this regard, but online dating is popular partly because since it's anonymous there's no accountability to someone like me.

Another reason it's popular is that it's simply so inexpensive compared to a personal matchmaker and takes little effort since you don't even have to get out of your jammies to meet a potential match. For those reasons, it may not attract the highest quality people or those truly looking for love, rather it may attract people just looking for sex or a way to feel good about themselves. Yes, most people report that online matchmaking just makes them feel *bad* about themselves (another reason I don't recommend it), there's a minority of people (often the very young, attractive, and shallow), who use it to give themselves a lift. Whether sex is involved or not, they'll ghost you before you can say boo!

Online dating might not create lasting relationships, but it does create situations where you can easily meet and date new people. Why get married when you can dive into a fun and exciting new relationship every few months? Or as your mother or grandmother might have said, "Why buy the cow when you can get the milk for free?"

Aditi Paul, the lead Michigan State researcher, surmised that there are three reasons why online relationships are less successful than those that start in real life:

1) App-dating provides people with too many choices. This means that individuals might find it difficult to be locked into one particular dating partner when

A word on 'the List' and online dating

App-based dating seems promising. You have the opportunity to look for someone who fulfills the qualities on your list. If your true passions are skydiving, abalone foraging, and snow camping, then you can probably find someone who has written a profile that's something kind of close to that. And when you find that online match, you're halfway to the altar!

Well … one Michigan State research study of 4,002 people found that couples who meet online are less likely to get married and more likely to break up than couples who meet in a face-to-face environment. Of course, this could be changing (the study was conducted between 2009 and 2013), but in my experience as a matchmaker I do find that in-person meetups are highly effective for meeting the *right* person, not just a person.

they know that literally hundreds of others — and maybe better ones! — are available anytime. It's a situation that may lead to delayed commitment.

2) Relationships initiated online take more time to develop, but not necessarily in a quality way — remember that "looking into each others' eyes" paragraph in the previous section? This may have to do with the trust issue. Eighty-six percent of online daters have reported being concerned about

potential falsification of personal information and deceptive self-presentation of their dating partners.

3) Paul also writes, "Even though a large percentage of marriages in recent years have resulted from couples meeting online, looking for partners online may potentially suppress the desire for getting married."

But that's not to say that online dating never works. Happy couples do indeed sometimes meet through internet dating sites. There are some good people who are serious about finding love on dating sites, along with the not-so-good ones, since it's popular and convenient. My advice?

1) *Don't use your real name for your screen name.* Pick a name that's evocative of your personality or lifestyle, such as "VeganSwimmer" or "CatDad." You don't need random people online to know your real name just yet.

2) *Be specific and truthful about yourself in your online profile.* This includes providing up-to-date photos that show you — not you in a group of friends, at a distance, wearing sunglasses or ski goggles, and so on. Being specific also means getting specific about what you seek, but not too specific. You don't want to miss out on someone just because they don't check every little box on your List.

3) *Try to meet the person as soon as possible to find out if they're legit and are who they represent themselves to be.* Also, from a chemistry standpoint, you want to make sure you enjoy the person's company and are attracted to them.

4) *Don't be a weirdo.* What I mean by that is don't make jokes that could be taken in the wrong way in your profile. In fact, try to avoid "jokes" while letting your natural zest for life and humor come to the surface. (It's a good idea to have your most normal or average friend read over your profile and look at the pictures to judge your attractiveness before you post it. (In addition to being "normal," your friend should be brutally, yet lovingly, honest).

Just your name, please. Don't use a "cute" email address, keep it simple using just your name. And please don't use a Yahoo, Hotmail, or AOL address, you'll seem hopelessly out of touch.

Don't use a family email account — I'm thinking specifically of the ones that contain your ex's or dead spouse's name. Yes, I really do have a stubborn client who insists on keeping the dead alive via an email address.

You never know how or when or where you'll meet your match, so you should be open and expand your search options, not limit them. Simply put, if you do choose to use dating sites, consider them just one tool in your toolbox. In other words, don't rely solely on online dating; go to social events, attend a church, temple, or synagogue, volunteer with a community organization, or otherwise get out of bed and out of the house, looking and smelling your best to be ready to meet new people. And don't forget to smile!

Your internet dating profile

Not everyone is comfortable doing online dating. Some don't want to do it because they think it's weird or impersonal, and you don't know if people are at all who they represent themselves to be. Others don't want to be on dating sites because they're well-known or, depending on what they do for a living, think twice about it. For example—teachers, professors, doctors, therapists, clergy—might not want the parents of their students, or their patients, students, or congregants—to see their profiles.

These days, it's a fact that the majority of single people will eventually log on to a dating site. There's no longer a stigma. It's quite a normal and natural way for people to meet and is more common than using a matchmaker with sites typically offering an initial free membership and then charging $10–$30 per month for membership. A matchmaker is generally $2,500–$5,000 a year and can go up to $200,000. Internet dating is certainly the economical route if money is a consideration.

I actually encourage my matchmaking clients to also be on internet dating sites, which is why I provide them profile advice at no extra charge.

Sometimes the smallest tweak to a dating profile can make all the difference in getting someone to notice them. Follow these guidelines and you'll have a much better response and be more likely to attract your kind of person.

Your photo is the most important marketing tool you have in internet dating. People sort through dozens, maybe hundreds, of profiles and you need to get their attention so they click on yours. A photo can make or break your chances of getting contacted, so make it a good one.

The Photo

Whether or not you look like a model, everyone can have attractive photos if you keep in mind a few key ingredients:

- Photos should be clear and good resolution, not blurry or grainy.
- Make sure the lighting is good.
- Make your main photo a headshot.
- Have the second photo be a full-length shot to show your physique, no matter how "good" or "bad" it is. You don't want potential matches to be surprised by your body when they meet you. Remember, for every different body type out there, there's someone who likes that body type. Really, there is.

- Make sure you have a warm, friendly smile in photos that show your teeth.
- Don't have other people in your photos. Definitely no photos with exes or photos that look like they have your exes cut out of them! No one needs to see your family, single friends, or coworkers with you. It's distracting, it can be confusing, and it's just not helpful in any way. You want prospective dates to focus on *you.*
- Wear clothes that flatter your body and show it off — but don't try to look like you just stepped out of a porn film or a "glamour" photo shoot. Men, don't go shirtless, please. Also, women really don't want to see you in your Speedo or dripping sweat at the gym, so be a bit modest in your selection of photos.
- Don't wear sloppy outfits or bulky clothes that make you appear heavier than you are. I see people showing off their winter vacation destinations with photos that show them bundled up in winter sweaters and thick jackets — not sexy! And it makes people look way bigger than they are. Show a little skin, just not too much. Make sure your hair is nice and the colors you wear are bright.
- Be sure to look right into the camera. It's said the eyes are the window to the soul. If you want to connect with someone, people need to see your eyes — no sunglasses!
- Lastly, if you can't manage to find a quality photo, then pay for a few professional ones. Photography is an art and a skill. Many people just don't have the ability to get all the

essentials with a friend or family member taking the shots. It's worth investing a bit for a few really great photos.

I helped get one client engaged just by telling him to switch out his profile pic. He thought he looked cool, but women wondered why he wasn't smiling. Men often have this mistaken idea not to smile and then it looks more like a mug shot. Just by putting him in a friendly pose showing off his beautiful smile and teeth, he was much more approachable. The dates followed.

If you don't post a photo, you won't come up in the majority of searches and few people will contact you or reply. A photo really is your most important way to get noticed among the many, many profiles.

Main Essay

Keep it short, positive, and light. There's a sales technique: "Be brief, be bright, be gone." Keep that phrase in mind as you *sell yourself* on your profile. You don't want to share your deep, dark secrets or disappointments with total strangers viewing your profile, and it certainly won't make you attractive to them. Anything you want to say that can be interpreted as negative, just flip it to the positive. If you say you're sensitive and brought to tears easily, some readers will think you're an emotional wreck or a neurotic mess. Instead, say something like you're a "caring, loving person." And beware of coded language. For instance, saying you're looking for a "generous" person is often code for a person who'll spend a lot of money on you. And "financially secure" means wealthy.

Don't talk about your past dating experiences or relationships or time on the dating app. Write only a short paragraph or two. People haven't even spoken with you yet, and they won't take the time to read a lengthy autobiography anyhow. Should you choose to share your life story on the app, remember: Anyone can read your profile. Anyone.

Leave money out of it. You can often guess a person's financial stability and economic class by other qualities, such as where they live, their profession, and their hobbies, without having to come right out with it. You don't want to attract shallow, materialistic gold diggers, do you?

Of course, even if you stay positive, you can still go wrong. For example, I had one client — a trim, attractive silver-haired gentleman — who went on and on in his profile about his four kids and 10 grandkids, and how much he loved to spend nearly every waking moment with them. Worse, every single photo in his profile featured him posed with the whole clan. You couldn't see his enviable physique or his well-put-together outfits for all the children climbing on him!

Needless to say, during his date-coaching session with me, I had to point out the obvious (which wasn't obvious at all to him): Spend a sentence or two on how much you enjoy being a grandfather—and then *get off the subject.* Then think of some other activities you enjoy. If you love to take your dog to the park, tell us about it. Use the tools of any good author by being specific and descriptive, and adding a touch of humor (but only if it comes naturally, otherwise your attempts at cornball comedy will only provoke groans on the other side of the computer screen). Share activities you do now or aspire to do with a special someone. Get creative. If you once went to Hawaii and learned to snorkel, talk about how you would love to return to the Big Island and enjoy the fishies with a partner.

In other words, you want to seem available. If you spend all your time with your grandchildren, or on your boat, at work, or at the golf course for that matter, then a potential mate will surmise that you won't have enough time to spend with them. You also want to make it clear that you are prioritizing the *search for romantic love* in your life. And finally, you want to convey a *fun-loving and sexy* persona — vibrant, interesting, and not burdened with a boatload of baggage.

A final note of caution on your essay: This is not the time to be poetic or sarcastic. You may think your artistic license is clever, but others, without context, will most likely just find it strange. You may think your sarcasm is funny or clever, but most people will just find it obnoxious. Besides, people reading your profile don't know you yet, so how will they even know what you write is meant to be sarcastic, anyway? They may just think you mean whatever negative or angry thing you just said. During my college days, I was a psychology research assistant for a study on "dominant and agreeable personalities." People who were sarcastic were perceived as dominant or aggressive; you want people to see you as agreeable — also known as *likable.*

Another note on social media, including dating apps that allow you to monitor how many people look at your profile: It may not be good for your state of mind. The fact of the matter is that studies over the years indicate that use of social media tends to be associated with increased social isolation. Although most of that research has been focused on kids and young adults, I believe there's nothing to negate

Profile checklist

- Don't wear sunglasses in your main photo. Show off your beautiful eyes.
- Don't use your real name in your profile.
- Don't be negative, especially about past relationships.
- Do have a native English speaker and friend read your profile for grammar and spelling, as well as a "weirdo check."
- Do be the only human in the photo. Dogs and cats are OK. They may even attract a fellow pet lover (or repel the allergic), which is really for the best anyway.

the idea that heavy social media use would affect adults any differently.

One study, published in the *American Journal of Preventive Medicine*, noted: "We are inherently social creatures, but modern life tends to compartmentalize us instead of bringing us together," according to lead author Dr. Brian A. Primack, Ph.D., director of the Center for Research on Media Technology and Health at the University of Pittsburgh School of Medicine. "While it may seem that social media presents opportunities to fill that social void, I think this study suggests that it may not be the solution people were hoping for."[1]

[1] Primack, Brian A. et al. "Social media use and perceived social isolation among young adults in the U.S." *American Journal of Preventive Medicine* 53, no. 1 (2017).

After studying more than 1,700 Americans ages 19 to 32, Primack's research team found that people who used social media for more than two hours per day saw twice the odds of perceived social isolation compared to peers who spent less than half an hour on social media each day.

The academics theorized that social media may contribute to perceived social isolation in various ways, including by inspiring jealousy and envy, and discouraging real-life interaction with loved ones.

More than a decade after the emergence of smartphones, Facebook, and Twitter, a profile is emerging of the "constant checker" — those who constantly check their emails, texts or social media accounts (43 percent of Americans). This attachment to devices and the constant use of technology is associated with higher stress levels for these Americans.[2] And no one needs that. Especially while trying to swim in the dating pool.

Table for one

I can't tell you how many of my clients are uncomfortable going to the movies or a restaurant alone, and so avoid it at all costs. Some have told me they haven't been to a movie theater in years! Come on, don't feel like the Steve Martin character in the 1984 movie *The Lonely Guy*. There's no spotlight and people aren't staring at you in real life. I always advise that you should really push yourself to venture out to activities without a friend or date.

---

[2] "Stress in America." American Psychological Association (2017). https://www.apa.org/news/press/releases/2017/11/lowest-point

Bring a book or text on your phone, or adopt a dog and dine in a place with a dog-friendly patio. (I'm going to say a lot about how adopting a dog can make you more attractive later in this section, because it really is true!) A dog will bless you with built-in company, and people who want to say hi to your pup. And not only will you save a dog's life, you'll also get more exercise walking your new doggie — something sure to help you be more toned and attractive. Whatever you do, don't feel you're doomed to eat takeout at home until you have a date to join you. You have nothing to be ashamed of, and have every right to go out and enjoy activities on your own. And you never know who you might meet while you're there or en route!

Where to meet someone

Be strategic. You're a unique person. You have passions, interests, things you care about, and things you like to do. *Be selective.* Don't spend time looking to meet random people at generic singles venues and events. Tailor your time to target people most likely to share your interests, values, lifestyle, or religion. Pick an internet dating app that has other people like you. Learn a new skill. Volunteer at a local nonprofit. Take classes, attend lectures, join intramural sports and activity clubs, go to meetups advertised online (if you don't see one that interests you, start one), travel with singles groups, or do a volunteer vacation program.

This doesn't mean you should rule out people who don't conform to your specs; it just means that you have limited time and energy, and you want to keep your spirits and enthusiasm up by not spreading your dating resume all over town. Going on a bunch of bad dates can be really demoralizing for people, especially for busy professionals — a serious waste of time. It's not true that "there are no good men or good women out there," you just need to look in the right places. For example, don't hang out in Napa Valley if you disapprove of drinking, don't live in Las Vegas if you're morally opposed to gambling, and for goodness' sakes, don't live in Montana if you're looking for a nice Jewish vegan gal.

Think you already know all the appropriate single people in your area? Keep in mind that you may simply know all the single people who go to "singles events." This is actually a *very small* percentage of single people. That's because these events don't tend to be very fun. Change up your routine, and you might just change your relationship status.

If you can work remotely, maybe move somewhere you've always liked on a short-term basis or do an intensive language study course abroad, or consider pitching in at an animal rescue center, food bank, or other charity of your choice. You never know what volunteers or language students you could meet who share your interests. Shake things up a bit: You never know how or when or where you'll meet your match, so try every avenue you can, and expand your search options. But remember, have fun doing it!

If you're not having fun, you quite simply will not have the stamina to persevere through the all-too-often-dispiriting dating game. Like finding a fulfilling job or your dream home, you wouldn't limit your search to one method, so when it comes to finding love, you should get creative and stay focused on the ultimate goal. Be determined to find your soul mate, and have faith that your true love is out there looking for you as well.

Missed connections

As I've mentioned, your soul mate may not come in the package you pictured, so be open to and aware of possibilities presented to you. Maybe this person doesn't have the education level, look, age, style of dress, or income you imagined. Maybe this person has an odd hobby, is divorced, has children, struggles to pay student loans, or has something else going on you never thought would be ideal. Maybe this person doesn't share your main interests, like your passion for cycling or taste in music. Still, if everything else is looking good, you probably should give the person a chance. After all, you don't need a carbon copy of yourself!

Here are some real-life examples of what I call "missed connections."

My client Cindy is 62 years old and divorced twice. She had these requests for the man I set her up with: Have him call me tomorrow between 8 and 9 am. Also tell him that I don't like to talk to people after 8 pm. I need to meditate for two hours before bed. I don't eat dinner. He'll have to take me to lunch.

One client, Ed, has been widowed for four years. He's 80 and lonely. But he won't date anyone out of his immediate area, anyone in *their* 80s, or anyone with a cane with a cane or a dog. He's not in great physical shape, so he won't date Angie who's into hiking and tennis, or anyone else too physically active, since he doesn't think he can keep up.

Shaun is 47 and has never been married. He waited two weeks to contact the woman I set him up with, then he texted her to ask when he could call the following week. I emailed him the advice to just call, since texting is so impersonal and doesn't elicit an emotional connection or romantic feelings, and it also makes him look too busy for a relationship. He replied "Good advice," then texted her again!

Janice, 45, also has never been married. In my opinion, she ruled out the perfect guy five years ago because he's only 5 feet, 8 inches. (She's 5 feet, 4 inches.) Who said the man has to be tall or taller than the woman?

I, for one, know lots of happy couples where the man is shorter than the woman or the same height. But this woman required her dates to be taller. And even though this man was technically taller than her, he was only 4 inches taller, and she wanted to wear heels and feel him towering over her. (OK, I'm not really sure what that's about. Far be it from me to analyze another person's hangups.) She wouldn't date a man unless he was at least 8 inches taller. Those are some really tall heels!

How much time do you spend standing next to your mate anyway? Isn't most of your time together as a couple going to be spent sitting or lying down? Janice seems like the nicest person; she looks great on paper, and she even volunteers for Habitat for Humanity. But she either rules out guys on paper, or is so critical and negative when meeting them that they're completely taken aback.

OK, so these superficial matters aren't really important, you may say . . . so what is? I believe the important thing is to be with someone who is nice to you and treats you with respect; someone who is trustworthy and loyal, whose company and conversations you enjoy; someone to whom you're physically attracted, and shares your deep goals, values, and overall lifestyle. You want someone whose touch you crave and whose body you desire. Your soul mate is your best friend and lover.

Some people become more set in their ways as they stay single, preferring to believe that they can order the perfect match like the old Burger King slogan, "Have it your way." I blame both app dating and the "shopping" for a mate it encourages, as well as self-help books that advise people to specifically visualize every detail about their goals, including that of their dream lover.

Now I'm not against knowing what's really important to you and even visualizing it, but the problem is when the List grows and grows and grows.

That's why the shopping that you see so often today for love matches is so often doomed. Although I'm not opposed to online dating or mass-market dating services, they too often encourage us to look at dating in the wrong way — as a series of boxes to check or leave blank.

Remember the '80s movie *Weird Science?* In the film, two teenage boys decide to create the perfect woman by plugging all their wants into a computer. Audiences laughed back then, but reality has caught up to the fantasy, and now grown men and women think that it's perfectly natural to enter all their wants into a computer, and presto! A dream partner will magically appear.

We use the check-boxes because they represent something we can measure and quantify. They represent guideposts for us, helping us to get to know ourselves while we continue looking for our match. They are the metrics for a part of life that is essentially unquantifiable and somewhat out of control. And once we meet the right person, we'll throw away the List. Our match will surely meet some of the important criteria, but he or she will also fail to measure up in innumerable ways — and it simply won't matter. After all, as Helen Keller wrote in the last century, "The best and most beautiful things in the world cannot be seen or touched. They must be felt with the heart."

Not everyone I meet is caught up in a computer-generated or visualized delusion. Others have actually learned from their time dating that the particular wants and needs that they may have had in their teens or 20s are not at all what's important now. As one guy told me recently, "In my 20s, I wanted a supermodel. Now, in my 40s, I realize that's not what makes a match."

Love isn't a group decision

Understand that your friends and family, despite appearances, may not always have your best interests in mind. Single friends may be jealous if you get into a relationship before they do, or want you all to themselves to go out on the town.

And your married friends may be the worst ones for giving love advice, because they are so far from the dating world. (Also, just because they're married doesn't mean they're happy or in good relationships.) And married friends may just want you coupled up. The point is that when you consider the points of view of others, also consider that they are invested in certain storylines that have nothing to do with your personal happiness. Some friends may be invested in you staying single, and other friends may be invested in you getting married. Family, especially parents, may be particularly invested in you getting married so that they "won't have to worry about you," either emotionally or financially. And, some parents may just want to have grandkids, no matter who you partner with.

Thinking outside the box

In the end, it's not about your family's approval, or impressing friends and strangers by parading someone around with good looks or status. What matters is how you feel when you're alone together, how this person treats you, how you feel when you're apart. Do you have mutual trust and respect? Do you laugh together? Enjoy conversation and company? Do you have a mutual sexual attraction? You deserve a best friend and lover, not just one or the other.

One of the reasons the divorce rate is so high is that many people marry the wrong person for the wrong reasons.

Your soul mate may come in a very different package than you ever pictured. Different than you ever imagined. How many people have you ruled out because they weren't a certain height, didn't have the right color hair, or much fashion sense? Didn't have the type of car you pictured or the type of profession. Or because he had a beard, was bald, or had long hair. She had freckles, or had short hair, or was a few pounds overweight, or was newly divorced, or had a young child. Not who you imagined your soul mate to be?

Not how you pictured your life? Maybe you need to shift your perspective.

To quote the Rolling Stones, "You can't always get what you want, [but] you get what you need." Don't be too rigid about your type and who you'll date, your soul mate may not look or be who you imagined. I can't tell you how frustrating it is as a matchmaker when I know I've got a great match for a client and they won't meet that person: They're not what my client pictured or have or don't have something "important."

One client refused to meet with a woman since she had a child. He said he tried dating women with kids and the children always got in the way of her attention for him. I assured him her teenager was living with his dad now, and about to go away to college, but this man wouldn't budge. He had set the idea in his head that he wouldn't date any more women with kids, due to a bad experience he had.

Well, I bet you're not surprised to hear that he's still single. Yes, many single parents have trouble making time for dating, but certainly not everyone, which is evident by the fact that many people with kids fall in love and remarry. My client ignored all the reasons why I might have had a perfect match and ruled the woman out since he was determined to stick to his guns on the issue of kids — even though her nearly grown son and her relationship with her son was different than the situation he'd experienced before with a woman and her kids.

Are these situations or characteristics what really matters for a soul mate connection? People often won't date anyone who's been divorced or doesn't have a college degree. Really? You don't know anyone who's been divorced for good reason and had a great and lasting second marriage? You can't think of anyone who is bright and successful without a degree? Let me tell you about Bill Gates and Oprah Winfrey then. I bet their significant others are glad they put the college degree issue aside. It's a real shame how many people miss out on life due to their own stubborn ideas, which can often get in the way of their happiness.

I always ask my clients for their ideal age range, look, and personality type they're attracted to. But I can't tell you how many people manage to rule out 90 percent of people due to overly limiting Lists, such as "must have blonde hair;" "can't be divorced;" "must live within a 30-minute drive of my home;" "parents must be married not divorced;" "must have an advanced degree;" "must have a degree from a top university;" "must be wealthy;" "must own a home;" "must be perfectly fit and thin;" "must be willing to move into my home."

Do you really want love? Your actions need to match your words.

Stay open to the possibilities, and don't sabotage yourself!

I've noted that you need to hang out in the right places to appeal to the kind of person you'd like to attract. I've also warned about approaching dating with a hard and fast list of qualities and requirements for a potential soul mate.

In fact, I find the List so unhelpful that in sharp contrast with many dating services and apps, I refuse to make my clients fill out a long, standard profile of what they want and their likes and dislikes.

I feel that the kinds of things that make people a match are the larger issues of trust, kindness, and mutual values. For many people, a match is entirely about physical attraction, and they go from there and try to figure the rest out later. Or on profiles, there are a lot of these generic questions, like age and location. For example, I have some people who call me and ask, "Do you have somebody who's in their early 30s, and this height, and wants this many kids, and lives in this area?" And I say, "Well yeah, I do, but it's going to take a lot more than that to make that person your match."

Be patient and open. You have to believe that they are out there and accept that the timing may be out of your control. I think the timing piece is hardest for people to accept, as love is about fate, and your soul mate might not be ready or available right when you want them to be. And it's essential to be open to love not coming in the package you pictured. Be flexible and be open about a personal "resume," in other words aspects like their location, if they've been divorced, their height, their exact physique, if they have children, their educational attainment, their profession, and so on. It's very important to be with someone you're attracted to and to be true to your values and goals, but the more superficial, limiting, and rigid you are about the List, the less likely you are to find love.

Also, for heaven's sake, don't rule out an entire class of people because of your stereotypes. For example, "I won't date lawyers" or "I won't date therapists." (Yes, clients have actually said these words to me.) That's a type of discrimination, and you're really missing out on the individual who is always the exception to the rule.

Of course, if people have it in their minds exactly what they're looking for, as a professional matchmaker, I'm going to respect their wishes. But I encourage clients to keep an open mind. If I think that two people share really deep values, and if they have looks that I think will go well together (more important to a soul mate connection than it ought to be, in my opinion), I think they should be willing to meet. They might just feel a connection.

If that person doesn't have the exact degree they had in mind, or the exact income, or the "right" height, or whatever it is, those things to me are not what necessarily make a lifelong match. (I don't even go into income when I speak with people, but sometimes they share.)

Don't invest time getting to know someone by phone or online, since everything can be over in a few minutes on a first date if there's no face-to-face chemistry. And you can get ruled out by sharing too much and not even get to have that first real date! It's too bad, since you might've been a good match in person. And everyone, if they're attracted to you, is more forgiving about everything on an actual date.

Unfortunately, thanks to the impersonal nature of talking on the phone, or reading an email, or viewing a dating profile, many people are quick to rule others out. Face-to-face is always best, so increase your odds at getting that chance of a first date by following my dating rules. (See **Dating Etiquette** sidebar.)

The phone call

But let me get back to the basics. How do you ask for that first date?

Dating Etiquette: 3 Rules of Engagement

1. Call to make the first date — don't email or text.
2. Make contact within a day or two to make the date. It's only going to be a five-minute call, so you don't need to wait till you've got a lot of time to talk.
3. Be mindful of the hour. Don't call during the day on weekdays to make the date; assume people are busy at work at that time. (Unless you know that they work unconventional hours as a night-shift nurse or bartender, for example — in which case don't call too early in the day, or you'll wake them up!) Don't call after 9 pm any day, unless of course you know they are just getting off work then. On weekends, don't call before 10 am. And don't call Friday or Saturday nights at all; even if you're not busy, you want to keep up the idea that you are.

Make the phone call to plan the first date really short and simple. Talk 5 or 10 minutes with the person at the most. Introduce yourself, say hello, tell them that you're looking forward to meeting, and make the plan. Get in and get out.

I recommend the phone because it's no longer the norm, and because of that it will certainly make you seem like a confident and caring person. In a sea of texts, it will help you stand out. Of course, if you know you're really awful on the phone, suffer from clinically paralyzing shyness, or have a truly awful voice, we can make an exception to the rule. Text away! But you better make those texts great, and follow the same rules of charming, polite efficiency.

Don't try to get to know each other or spend weeks on the phone, and definitely don't let weeks go by before you meet. Another client of mine shared her past medical problems on the initial setup phone call, because her date asked her how she got into her profession as a yoga teacher. Her date didn't want to meet her after that. Even though I had advised her against it, she shared all of the details.

In a case like this, I would counsel people to share, but like any good PR person, "Stay on message!" I reminded her that she simply could've said how she decided to make a change toward a more healthful lifestyle without mentioning the health issues that led to her becoming a yoga instructor. There are lots of truthful details she could have included without telling him the medical problems part. It just wasn't his business in this initial phone call, and she shouldn't have felt obligated to tell him about it.

Just because someone asks doesn't mean you have to answer. They don't really want to hear your whole life story, anyway. Really they don't. You can joke that you're out of dating practice and been advised everyone's told you not to talk too long before the date. Or, if you're not new to dating, you can be a little flirtatious and say that's what the date is for and you're looking forward to getting to know them Tuesday, or whenever the date is.

Now if they overshare with you, see if you can redirect the conversation. For example, if your prospective date begins telling you about their deceased spouse. Let them know that you too had a wonderful marriage — if that's the truth — but that's a part of your past, and you're here to get to know them and focus on the present.

There are lots of polite ways to respond to people's inappropriate questions or statements. It's a lot easier to do if you keep the call short and just make the date. If the person on the other end of the phone gets too chatty, in a friendly tone, tell them you need to go but look forward to meeting them and continuing the conversation in person.

Taking a snapshot

That first phone call is a snapshot of your life. Meaning whatever you share, the person on the other end of the phone will generalize that this is representative of your life and how it is most of the time. So if you're in a bad mood from something that happened at work, or had a fight with your mom, or have a headache or whatever, your date will think that's how it usually is in your life. They will jump to conclusions, since they're not invested and don't know you well enough to give you the benefit of the doubt. And, even if you don't want to, you'll likely generalize the same way about them.

Again, don't text in general at the start, but of course, if your date is coming up, feel free to text the address of where you're going to meet or some other key bit of information. This type of info is best conveyed in writing for reference.

Look your best and make a good first impression

You don't have to have a perfect body or have a face like a model to find love; your soul mate will be your type, and you will be theirs. You never know how or when or where you're going to meet your soul mate, so be ready! Look nice even

Let Your Fingers Do the Calling

Call! Don't text! Don't expect a person to feel romantic about you when the only contact you've had is a text to set up the date, and a few more texts to work out the details. Your voice can be sexy. Talking creates connection. Texts do not. You seem lazy, busy, or disinterested if you don't call. And texts don't necessarily save time. There are few things more annoying than spending hours setting up a potential date via text when a three-minute phone call would have done the trick.

Then, if you're interested, call the day after the date to say what a great time you had. Call in-between the next date just to say hi and see how they're doing. Getting to know each other and making a connection is a way to build romantic feelings — or to rule each other out before you've invested too much time.

Talking is the best way to get to know each other and by doing it over the phone or by videochat, you're less likely to rush into sex and possibly regret it. Talk and talk some more to see if you share what matters: values, goals, lifestyle. And a note on videochats: Please don't surprise your date with a Facetime call. Your date will want to look their best for a Facetime or Zoom call, and it's just bad manners to sneak attack like this.

Of course there's a place for texting, but don't rely on it exclusively.

I had a client wait two weeks to contact a woman I wanted him to meet. Instead of calling, he texted her — wanting to set a time for a call in the next couple of weeks after he returned from vacation. Of course, she was not impressed that he let so much time go by and then his first contact with her was by text. If you're too busy to find five minutes for a call, your potential date will think you certainly don't have time for a relationship.

So just pick up the phone to make the date. Keep the call friendly but brief, and keep the focus on scheduling the date.

when walking your dog or going to the store. I don't mean dress for a cocktail party or a job interview to work out or run an errand, but look decent and well groomed, with your hair and clothes nicely put together at a minimum.

Work on your outer and inner well-being, in general, to be your best self — healthy, fit, attractive. Keep your hairstyle nice, exercise, eat healthy, whiten your teeth if they're yellow from drinking coffee or red wine, moisturize your skin. Women: I always advise wearing some minimal, natural-looking makeup, including eyeliner, lipstick or gloss, mascara (if you've got light eyelashes), and a little blush. Note that heavy makeup can actually make you look older, and also ridiculous if not worn in the right setting or with a more formal evening outfit. Buy some new clothes (they don't have to be expensive!) that can be your go-to ensemble to look put together and stylish for any occasion. Before cutting off the tags, ask for input from your most stylish — and truthful — friend or family member to confirm the outfits are both in fashion and flattering on you. Have a positive attitude. Be agreeable, hopeful, happy, optimistic, and open to opportunities that present themselves to you.

Smile! It's such a simple way to be more attractive. When you smile at someone, they almost always smile back and feel good no matter their mood. Social psychologists have done studies on people's facial expressions and how they transmit feelings to others. It turns out that smiles are contagious, just like yawns. You look happy and friendly when you smile, and people are attracted to happy, friendly people.

Individuals are drawn to nice people, and a person with a warm smile is much more appealing than someone who looks angry or unhappy or just disinterested. How many times have you seen attractive people who seem unapproachable or not that nice, simply because of the expression on their faces? Then they smile at you and you're comfortable and they become even more attractive. Or maybe you can recall times when you've seen people who are plain-looking but light up the room because of their big, friendly smiles and the twinkle in their eyes. They smile like they mean it — and the smiles ricochet back to them.

And smiling can actually *change your mood,* making you more truly happy. You smile and you feel good.

A book called *How to Make Anyone Fall in Love with You* (great title, right?) relates a story that the television newsmagazine *20/20* once did, which supposedly tested the willingness of strangers to help out an attractive woman stranded with her car on the side of the road. Two women, both actresses, were filmed. Both of them were fairly attractive. Yet one of the women literally stopped traffic, while no one bothered to help the other one. What was the first woman's secret? She *acted* attractive and friendly by smiling, establishing eye contact as the drivers approached, and threw her head and shoulders back. The other woman *acted* miserable and crossed her arms over her chest, not bothering to smile or look at the drivers whizzing by.[3]

So start with a smile and add other friendly body language as you become more comfortable with dating and

---

[3] Leil Lowndes, *How to Make Anyone Fall in Love with You* (New York: McGraw-Hill Education, 1997)

flirting. As you become more interested in a person, signal that interest with a touch on the arm, deep eye contact, and a warm hug — and maybe even a little kiss when you say goodbye.

What should you do on a first date?

I have a lot of people who ask "What should I do on a first date?" Well, it really doesn't matter that much, although you do get extra credit for thinking up something relatively interesting that says something about your personality. But this is not the TV show *The Bachelor*, so nothing too long, expensive, or complicated. What's more important than what you do is to make the first date short and simple, or again, *Be brief, be bold, and be gone!*

Make time to meet the person and keep the date casual, relatively short, and inexpensive. Meet at a quiet bar or coffee shop, or go for a walk somewhere public, anywhere where it's not going to take a lot of time and expense. Spend about an hour for the date, at the most. And, leave if you're having a bad time. You're under no obligation to stay a set amount of time.

This first date is just to see if there's any point of connection, to see if you want to go out again. I advise everyone to not overshare: Don't talk about exes (this includes child custody battles, cheating, nightmare stories of a crazy ex, or even the fact that you're best friends with your ex — they'll picture the ex always around or worry about you cheating), dead spouses (your wonderful, successful, perfect spouse), dating life (dating app woes, tales from singles events, and so on), money problems (student loan debt, bankruptcy, that time you were fired, the bad investment you made that resulted in a mountain of credit card debt), or health problems (no stranger wants to imagine life as your caregiver). Essentially avoid anything that is personal, heavy, negative, a downer, or could be used by your date to draw negative conclusions and make judgments about you. Trust me, it will be held against you. Imaginations run wild in the absence of information.

Recently, a new client told me he shared personal stuff about his deceased spouse while on a date because his date asked. She wanted to know how long he was married and how long it had been since his wife had died, so he told her. She ended up not wanting to see him again because she decided he wasn't ready to date and that he needed more time to mourn the loss. This was all based on something she was told by her therapist, as if everyone had the same marriage, the same loss, and grieves the same way. I found it very insulting and arrogant for this person to decide for her date that he's not ready to explore a new relationship.

One widower client spent a first date talking about finding his wife fallen in the shower after a stroke. There was blood everywhere and she was in a coma for a month before she died. Once he told this story, his date just could not get the image out of her head. There was no second date.

On a lighter note, one of my favorite episodes of the TV show *Veep* is called "Library." In it, a male character goes on a blind date. On the date, he talks about how the doctors dealt with his cancerous testicle by removing it. Gross!

If that wasn't enough, he then told his date that she

could only have two courses at dinner: "You can have a main and an appetizer or dessert, but not both." Then he asked to see a current photo of her mother: "I'm going to need both a front and a rear." Charming!

Seriously, though, whether it's a coffeehouse or wine bar date, a walk in the park, or a short hike, keep it brief. I had a date-coaching client tell me she and her date were both hard-core hikers so they went on a 15-mile hike on their first date. No, no, no! After about an hour, they realized liking each other's photos and having a mutual interest in hiking was not enough to be a love match. They were stuck with each other in the middle of nowhere all day!

Even if you both love a certain activity, if you choose to do it for the first date, make sure to make it an abbreviated version. And choose an activity for your first two or three dates where you can talk, not something where your focus is elsewhere or you have to be quiet, like a movie, lecture, play, or concert. After the first date, feel free to meet for a meal. Whether meeting for a drink or taking a walk, I highly recommend keeping the first date casual and under an hour.

In short, just make plans for a light and simple date to see if you like each other enough to go on a second date.

Before the date

Congratulations, you have a date! This is the point at which I tend to think of the famous Louis Pasteur quotation, "Fortune favors the prepared mind." Except I replace "mind" with "person."

Please show respect for both your date and yourself by

taking just a few extra minutes to prepare yourself for the date. Even if the setting is casual, there's no reason to show up late or frazzled. Triple-check that you know the directions and leave enough time to get to the meeting place, and know where you'll park when you get there. If parking isn't easy, just suck it up and pay a few bucks to park in a nearby lot. Navigation apps make this easy. Again, make sure you have extra time to arrive early, so you're relaxed and not rushing in. It's easy to be nervous on a date, so you want to make sure you can be as relaxed and composed as possible.

It's showtime, folks!

I'd like to tell you a little bit about how to present yourself on a first date. I get a lot of people asking me about attire, especially if they are following my advice and going to a casual place like a coffee shop or maybe even taking a walk in the park.

My opinion is that even if it's your day off and you like to dress very casually, as people on the West Coast tend to do, that does not mean you wear a T-shirt and sweatpants. Please people, step it up a bit and put yourself together. Just as you would in a job interview, where you really want to dress nicer than anybody who's interviewing you, you want to dress nicer than the majority of people sitting around in that coffee shop. Make a good first impression, and get an opportunity for a second date.

So dress a little sexy, show a little skin, wear nice jewelry. Jeans are okay, but make sure they are fashionable, well-fitting ones, and make sure your upper half is a little fancy. Men:

Wear a button-down shirt, polo shirt, or sweater. Women: Wear a nice sundress or feminine top and accessories. Be tasteful and make your date feel like you cared enough to make an effort. If you wear flip-flops, don't take them off and put your bare feet up on a chair next to your date! This happened with a client of mine. Needless to say, she wasn't interested in seeing him again. Not a way to impress.

Be well-groomed. If you have a beard, make sure it's trimmed, check your hair and face in the mirror (see that there's nothing in your teeth or nose) before you go to meet the person, take a breath mint or chew a piece of minty gum in advance of meeting your date — and then get rid of it; you don't want to be chomping away at your meeting. Again, make sure you have a nice smile on your face, make casual eye contact, and really listen.

As I've mentioned before, make sure to ask your date questions about themselves and show interest in their answers. Too often, I hear from clients that their date talked all about themselves during the meeting, that the date didn't seem to want to hear anything about the other person in the room. I can't convey to you what a huge turnoff that is. Most people will think you're a great conversationalist if you just listen.

Dating Hack

Show interest in the other person by asking them questions about themselves — not in relation to your List, but real questions that signal you're interested in getting to know them better. Most people love to talk about themselves if they're presented with a willing and engaged audience. Be that audience.

Some people insist that a first date involves a meal, but I recommend that the first date be just for drinks at a relatively quiet cafe or coffeehouse rather than a lengthy or expensive meal. Having multiple drinks at a noisy bar isn't a good idea for a host of reasons (expense, lack of judgment, difficulty in talking) and, as I've mentioned, cocktails and dinner isn't a great idea either, because if you don't like each other you'll be stuck with that person for hours — and stuck with a big tab too.

Now it's tempting to try to wow a potential mate on a first date with something really creative: apple-picking at an orchard out of town, a visit to the county fair, or a day at the Nascar track, for example. And while I don't say never plan an interesting date (dating would become quite a slog otherwise), do keep in mind that many of the more involved plans require a major time commitment. So unless you have a really good feeling about that first date, don't commit to an all-day activity; once you meet that person, the last thing you want may be to hang around together without an escape hatch! I generally recommend that you leave the longer, more involved plans for the second date. Of course, always make sure you are in a public place the first few times you meet a new person. No matter what you choose to do as an activity, your personal safety should be a priority.

Stay Safe on Your Date

- Keep your personal information private
- Go at your own pace
- Always meet in public
- Trust your instincts
- Never share financial information

Is it OK to cancel?

Ideally, honor your dating commitments. But every once in a while, *rescheduling* a date is best for everyone.

For example, I have a client I was sure was perfect for the woman I set him up with, but on the day of their first date, he came down with a raging migraine. He thought it would be rude to postpone the date, but the truth is there are some times when there are really good reasons for canceling a date and rescheduling — like getting bad news that day, or in his case, a migraine.

You only have one chance to make a good first impression, as they say, so you want to be at your best. So don't show up on a date like he did, clothes disheveled and your hair a mess. He couldn't even focus on what his date was saying, because he was in so much pain. Sadly, because he tried to man up for her sake, she thought he just wasn't that interesting of a guy and she didn't give him a chance for a second date.

A more recent example is that of a doctor who showed

up on no sleep after being on call all night at the hospital. *This would have been a great time to reschedule!* Rescheduling is not only for your benefit, but also out of respect to your date who presumably put effort into preparing for the meetup. If you're too tired, too sick, or too distracted to focus on conversation, there's really no point to the date.

Just be up front with the person. For instance, "I'm so sorry, I'm not feeling well. I need to reschedule the date." They know you are serious, you're not blowing them off, you're not being a flake, and you have a legitimate reason for needing to postpone.

But what if you don't just want to postpone — you actually want to *cancel*? You've thought about the match too much, you've taken a second look at their profile, or you had an awkward phone call. You just don't think that the date is going to go anywhere. Of course, you have to trust your instincts, but I usually advise people to *just go on the date.*

After all, there was something there that initially sparked your interest in this person. Why should you overthink the situation and cancel a first date before you've even met your potential match? You know people don't actually look as good in a photo, they don't necessarily sound as good on the phone, they don't necessarily express themselves well via text. What really matters is having a connection in person. That's one reason I suggest that you not spend too much time getting to know each other by phone or via text. You don't want to rule each other out before you meet — and conversely you don't want to get too excited before you meet — because it can all be over in five minutes if there's no real chemistry, attraction, or connection in person. *So please, just go on the date.*

Is it OK to date someone newly single?

If you don't, somebody else will! The circumstances of a newly single person are unique to that individual. Whether the person is newly separated, divorced, or widowed, who are you to determine or judge when they're ready for a new relationship? They certainly know themselves better than you do.

There are no hard and fast rules about how long it should take to get over a loss of someone or a broken heart. Every relationship is different and everyone feels and responds differently to loss. And if they chose to end the relationship, they're likely to be ready to move on right away.

If someone says they're ready and you don't feel they are, based on them talking about the past relationship too much or sending other clues, then discuss it with them and make your own decision about whether you want to date that person, but at least take the time to listen.

A caveat on chemistry

Now I've mentioned that chemistry is of the utmost importance to a relationship, but I feel that I should explain myself a bit more in that area. I've actually seen two types of chemistry in my matchmaking work, and you should be aware of them both.

The first type is the classic, "love at first sight" fireworks: You both feel a strong attraction immediately upon meeting each other and you just want the date to go on and on. When you finally do have to part, you can't stop thinking about each other and can hardly stand it until you see each other again. Does this really happen anywhere but the movies? Why yes, of course it does! And if you experience it, by all means, throw all my guidelines out the window and see where this budding connection leads.

What about love at first sight?

You won't know if it's real until you get to know each other and see how you are together over time. How does this person treat you and make you feel when life gets stressful and unpredictable things happen — rather than just being fun on dates.

But there's another type of chemistry I've seen. I call this the *slow burn* type of chemistry, and it's a lot more difficult to gauge. The truth is, I can't tell you how many happily married couples didn't feel much of a connection on the first or even second date. So I strongly encourage you to give someone a second or even a third date as long as you have a reasonable amount of time in your life and aren't turned off by their looks, and have plenty in common as far as lifestyle, values, interests, and goals.

Trust me: For a variety of reasons, chemistry is often not apparent on the first date. For many couples, a strong chemistry develops as the two people get to know each other more deeply over time. Think back to the beginning of this book. Remember my first match? I knew that my friends were soul mates, but I had to push them to go out again: Neither one was particularly excited by their first date. They tried again and the second date did it. They've been happily married for fifteen years, are super in love, and have two wonderful children. Even though they felt no fireworks at first, they ended up a match made in heaven.

I tell this story to many of my clients who call me after a first date that didn't result in immediate fireworks. Although I would never advocate going on date after date with a person that doesn't make your heart flutter, I do regularly urge clients to give a potential match one or two more tries, just to make sure there's not something deeper there that could be overlooked on first impression.

Put in a little effort

If someone's driving far to meet you, be sure to do your research to pick a coffee shop or other place to meet — don't make them suggest the place. With the magic of the internet, there's no excuse for not knowing where to meet these days, even if you're based in a city you don't know well. And be sure to pick up the tab for their drink or snack! Remember, they put in a lot of effort to meet you, you can expend a little effort for them.

Don't Ask!

Avoid any questions about:

1. Health
2. Wealth
3. Drugs
4. Sex

What to say (and not say) to get a second date

I like the dating and relationship advice I once saw from a group of elementary school kids. I was taken by one little boy's response to the question, "How would you make a marriage work?" And I think it applies to dating as well. Joe, age 10, advised: "Tell your wife she's pretty, even if she looks like a dump truck." 'Nuff said, Joe.

I think that Joe's advice is really summed up by the credo: *Don't be judgy!* One female client went on a date with a doctor who works seven days a week. She kept telling him that she couldn't believe he didn't own an SUV to haul camping gear and home renovation supplies around (as she did). Mentioning a difference is fine, but to say the same thing five times just served to make the guy feel like she thought he wasn't masculine enough for her.

I always encourage clients to be direct with each other on dates, but *delicate* honesty really is the best policy. Unfortunately, this is a difficult concept for some people. Because of that, and until a client gets their dating sea legs, I will sometimes step in and handle certain uncomfortable situations, such as when someone has gone on a first date and isn't interested in a second. By dealing with these situations over many years, I really do think I've heard it all.

Show some enthusiasm!

I had a client who said she had a really nice time on her first date with a guy I set her up with. They enjoyed a lively conversation, had a lot in common, and he was pleasant to be around. At the end of the date, he walked her to her car, told her he had a nice time, and asked her if it would be okay if he called her because he'd like to see her again.

She replied with "sure," and then held out her hand to shake his. The next day, he left a message on her voicemail that on second thought he didn't think they should go out again after all. She appreciated his candor and direct communication, but she was befuddled about his change of heart.

When she called me to report on how the date went, I pointed out that the handshake quashed any warm, let alone romantic, ending to the date. Furthermore, instead of her giving an enthusiastic response to his inquiry about seeing him again, like "Sure! That would be great!" or "I had a really good time and would love to see you again," she came off as lackluster and somewhat disinterested by saying simply, "Sure."

Remember that more often than not like attracts like. If you smile, you will be greeted with smiles in return. If you're eager to see someone again, they will be eager to see you again. And if you play it too cool, you might just get iced out.

... But don't come on too strong

One man I know went on a date with a woman, and they liked each other enough to plan a second date. But first, she was going on vacation. He remembered the exact day that she would return, and he called the morning after she returned to plan date *número dos.* She was impressed! They decided to go to dinner and a movie the next weekend. All good so far.

But here's where things began to go awry. Between the planning of the date and the actual date, he called her every day, five days in a row. By midweek, she told him that she didn't really like talking on the phone. Still, our hero was undaunted, and continued to call. By the weekend, she cut off the date after the movie, choosing to skip out on dinner. Needless to say, he was very disappointed.

How to explain her behavior? And does she really hate the phone? The point here is that the guy came on way too strong and didn't listen to his paramour's signals — at all. He was being pushy with a woman that he barely knew. And there's nothing less attractive to a person than a date who seems more interested in the idea of being in love than listening and getting to know the actual person who they claim to be interested in.

You can get away with sending more texts than phone calls, but even a text a day (even if they are just funny cat GIFs) can be pretty annoying. *Read the signals.* Unless you are getting multiple calls, emails, and texts back, don't do it! If you are always the one that initiates, and continues contact, just cool your heels and give the relationship time to progress.

Besides seeming weird and borderline stalkery, you simply don't want to exude any level of desperation in your communication. I'm convinced that we are all biologically wired to be attracted to what is maybe a little bit mysterious and seemingly unattainable and repelled by what is too familiar and comes too easily.

I thought of this again recently while watching *Seinfeld* reruns. In a variation of the old Groucho Marx joke, "I don't want to belong to any club that would accept me as a member," George didn't think anyone who would date him was good enough. I tend to see this phenomenon most at play when therapists won't date therapists, lawyers won't date lawyers, or filmmakers and actors won't date entertainment-industry types.

I think that our perfect matches tend to be in the gray zone in which we date someone whom we think is just a little too good for us, whether it's too pretty or handsome, too intelligent or worldly, or too sensitive and kind. The magic trick is to find someone who thinks *you* are too good for them while you think *they* are also too good for you.

When it comes to asking about a second date, you don't want to play games. You don't want to wait a week, or two weeks, or whatever it may be, to call that person and make the connection to set up the date. Yes, I said call again. You may think that I'm hopelessly old-school, but I really find that a quick call goes a long way in proving to a potential partner that you're interested in and serious about them. Texts have their place, and can be really fun and flirtatious after a few dates, but nothing gets the ball rolling and telegraphs seriousness about a potential partner than a well-placed call.

Call right away. I would say within a day or two call that person, show that you're reliable, that you're interested, that you're serious. There are lots of flaky game players out there, but that's not what you're interested in and (we hope) that's not what they're interested in. If you're sincere about finding love, you want to call that person right away.

I have had several clients really ruin their chances because even though they had good intentions, they waited to call the person until they thought they had a good chunk of time to speak. They put off calling for a week, two weeks; I've even heard three, four, five, or six weeks! By the time they got around to calling that person, he or she had either forgotten about them or was so annoyed it was useless. And that's really a shame. They might have been a good match. So I really encourage you and I can't overstate it enough, just call. It only needs to take five or ten minutes to plan a second date. Remember that the in-person meetups are what's important, not talking endlessly on the phone or trading texts half the day.

Meet, meet, meet

This goes for my matchmaking clients as well as people who are doing app-based dating or blind dates of any kind. The reason why you want to use the phone or the internet as little as possible — preferably for simply setting a date, place, and time to meet — is that dating involves a heavy dose of chemistry, something that you simply will not be able to gauge over the phone, or by email or text. Therefore, why waste your time getting into a relationship with a person you may not like in the flesh, or vice-versa?

This idea was brought home to me after I set one of my clients up with a woman he was really excited about. Because he lives in San Diego and she lives in Portland, it seemed natural to them that they get to know each other on the phone before meeting. But after two months of "dating" each other exclusively over the phone, they still hadn't met even though the guy had offered to fly up multiple times. Although he felt very attached to her and she said she felt the same, he finally asked me if he could be set up with some other women.

What was going on here? He wasn't sure why she seemed to put off meeting him, whether it was her work life or her single motherhood, but this phone relationship finally got to him, and what seemed a match seemed doomed before it even got interesting. They wasted emotional energy getting attached, invested lots of time on lengthy calls, and meanwhile, may have missed out on meeting someone else who may have been "the one," or at the least, was willing to make time for a first date and eventually a relationship.

Keep an open heart

I've mentioned this in previous sections, but it bears repeating: Try not to be judgmental about potential dates. (It helps if you try to slow down your general level of judgyness about everyone in your daily life.) I know that you may be going on a date that you believe won't work out because a relative, coworker, or friend suggested it, or you just don't want to stay home alone on a Saturday night. But just be aware that these feelings, even if you're sure you are putting on a good front, will come out on the date somehow — be it via your body language, through a comment you might make, or simply through the general vibe you put off.

Yes, attitude matters. That's why I encourage you to really put the chapters on ***Desire*** and ***Belief*** into action before you dive head first into the dating pool. It's absolutely critical that you're not only ready to accept another person into your life, but that you've done your inner work to become the kind of person that attracts the person you need (notice that I didn't say *want)* into your life.

I once had a client, a very thin and fit-looking attorney whom I set up with a nice-looking guy with a trimmed beard and beautiful eyes. He was carrying a few extra pounds around in his belly area, and unfortunately, he chose to order french fries on their first date. She stuck to a simple glass of white wine, declining his offer to share his fries with her. She didn't say anything about the fact that he unapologetically ate a plate of fries on the date, but her face said more than she intended.

I talked to them both over the phone after their date. Although she was turned off by his tummy, she liked him quite a bit and knew that she shouldn't feel so judgmental about a guy liking his fried food. Sadly, the guy wasn't sure he liked *her.* Sure, she was pretty and fit, but she came off as cold and unloving. He just didn't get the impression she really liked him, so a second date never happened.

While it's a great idea to visualize letting someone into your life, and knowing what are crucial qualities, having a too-detailed list of your requirements can be self-defeating.

First, there is the danger that you will stay single. I can't tell you how many men I meet who are in their sixties and are still looking for the perfect twenty- or thirty-something to "give them" children. At the same time, I've also met women who are now in their fifties or sixties who, in their fertile years, passed up men who were perfect in every way but who didn't want children; unfortunately many of them never found the right mate and never had children regardless.

Second, there's the very real possibility that you end up with someone who is "good on paper," but is a horrible match for you. In love, as in sports, not every quality ends up on your stat sheet. Chemistry counts — a lot — and will make up for a lack in many areas you thought you needed. Mind you, chemistry isn't just sexual attraction. I'm also talking about those elusive qualities that allow you to have endless conversations, sit quietly in comfort, or know what the other person is thinking without ever speaking.

Every pot has a lid that fits; in other words, there's someone for everyone. You think you're too short, too fat, too tall, too old, too uneducated, too poor, too whatever. Others may seem prettier, more successful, luckier — more deserving of love. It's just not true. Love is not a competition. There's no shortage of single people in the world, even though it may feel that way sometimes. Just take a look at the millions of people on dating sites if you don't believe me!

Remember that you need to expand your search options to expand your pool of possibilities. The right one is out there for you, and they will see you for who you are and will want you just the same. You have to believe you're worthy of love, that you deserve to be loved. You don't have to be a perfect person. You'll be the perfect one for your soul mate.

Pet the pooch

If you want to woo someone, pay attention to their pet! If they bring a dog on the date and you barely touch or even notice Fido, you will not score points. Show interest in the one they love if you want them to love you.

At the same time, research shows that pet caretakers in general are perceived as better catches than those who don't have pets. According to a 2015 study of 1,210 cat and dog guardians published in the journal *Anthrozoös,* about 30 percent of people said that they had been "more attracted" to someone who had a pet, while more than half said they would find someone more attractive if they knew the person had *adopted* a pet. Furthermore, more than 50 percent of respondents said they would not date someone who did not like pets; and about two-thirds of respondents said they would judge their date based on how they responded to their own pet.

Men, take note, the results were even more pronounced for women than men. And the results were starker still when it came to dogs as romantic barometers.

According to an article published in the *New York Times* in 2018, studies show that people rank others as happier, safer, and more relaxed when they appeared with a dog in a photo, as opposed to being pictured alone. The article went on to say that experiments also indicate that men have more luck getting a woman's phone number if they ask while they have a dog with them.

Are pet guardians actually better relationship material? Those that care for pets certainly think so. In a series of studies, Canadian researchers Anika Cloutier and Johanna Peetz (not to be confused with "petz") showed that more than 86 percent of pet caretakers believed that their pets had a positive effect on their relationships. The researchers posited that "a pet might provide the opportunity to practice empathic abilities, which is a crucial ability in the maintenance of positive relationships." How long you've had a pet may also matter. Cloutier and Peetz's results showed that the number of years an individual owned a pet was positively correlated with empathic concern, which in turn was linked to several relationship benefits (commitment, couple identity, and "relationship maintenance behaviors").

Which comes first, the pet or the good relationship? It's hard to say. After all, you're probably not going to get a dog or cat with a partner unless you're pretty serious about that person. But at the same time, if you can't commit to walking a dog or feeding a cat, you might not be ready to show up for your beloved either.

In my personal work, I've certainly found that women really do judge men favorably for being a good dog dad. However, I've also seen something troubling that these studies don't explore: Unfortunately, a number of my clients have been in the situation where the men are *jealous* of the woman's dog rather than attracted to her for having one. I even had one male client try to get a match I made to give up her dogs for him! (Always a bad idea — unless there's a serious allergy involved, and even that's debatable if it's controlled by medication.)

I know another woman who is a serious animal lover who fostered and then adopted a disabled street dog from Mexico. That dog was sweet and submissive, but it immediately exposed some serious cracks in the woman's serious, live-in relationship. Her boyfriend, while loving and wonderful in many ways, simply *did not like dogs,* and really believed that pets should live outdoors (and certainly not on beds or sofas). The woman couldn't believe that her boyfriend wouldn't fall in love with the new rescue, but he didn't. She realized that if she couldn't have pets with this man, this relationship clearly had no future. She finally moved out, and into an apartment with a group of five dog-loving friends. She now spends her free time skiing, rock-climbing, and volunteering with the local SPCA. Although not particularly focused on finding a new partner, I'm convinced that it's just a matter of time before she meets an athletic, animal-loving Mr. Right.

What's the Rush?

Don't introduce your prospective mate to your family, especially your parents or kids, right away. But do let them meet your dog or cat. After all, you need to know if your pet doesn't like your new love … they likely have good reasons.

Maybe those men who are competing with a pup simply fall into the "no wonder you're still single" category. But it's hard to say without real research. Who knows? There may actually be something that some dogs and men share from a biological perspective that makes them need to be the "alpha" in a woman's life.

> **Man, Get a Dog!**
>
> Adopt a dog, dude! Women are attracted to men who have dogs, especially if the dogs are rescues. To women who love dogs, the presence of a pooch can show that a man is able to commit to loving and being responsible for someone other than himself — and do it on a schedule. In other words, perfect dad material.

How to say goodbye: Two ways

You have to clearly communicate your interest and intentions — or your disinterest — even as soon as the first date. For example, is your long-term plan to get married? I recently got an email from a woman, who recapped her first date this way: "He is a lovely human being. I'm really grateful that you set me up with him because he is a complete gentleman and did nothing wrong on the date. I'm just a little worried, because he didn't seem interested in getting married and I get confused about whether a man can commit to a woman and not marry her." (For the record, *he can.*)

For what it's worth, I replied that lots of people can commit without getting married. After all, it's better to be officially single and in a committed relationship than married to the wrong person. And it's important to realize that a problem with commitment is not the same as not wanting to get married.

If you want to see the person again: Smile warmly, say something like, "This was fun. I really enjoyed meeting you." If you're shy about suggesting another date, stop there and gauge the other person's response, giving them a chance to ask you on another date. If you're feeling bold, or if you think the other person's shy, continue on and just say it: "I'd love to see you again."

This is where it gets tricky. Some folks may become uncomfortable and say something they don't mean, like "That sounds great — I'll call you!" when they have no intention of doing so and no desire to see you again. All you can do is take them at their word, but don't forget to pay attention to body language — does he move to give you a warm hug, does he smile, does he seem genuine when he says he'll call?

If you don't *want to see the person again:* I always suggest that you say it straight out in a respectful and polite manner. "It was nice meeting you, but I don't think we're a match." However, clients often tell me that doing this is extremely difficult. So I propose an alternative. Offer a hand for shaking and say, "It was nice meeting you. Take care." The handshake takes any romantic potential out of the goodbye, making the transaction more like the end of a business meeting than a date. Paired with the generic phrase, your date should get the message: "See you never ever. Have a nice life."

Be Clear If You're Not Interested

Just tear off the Band-Aid already! You're not doing them any favors by saying you'll call or would like to see them again if you have no intention of ever doing so. It's actually kind of cruel to have somebody waiting for your call or leaving the calendar open for a second date, while you merrily go on to other dates and never look back.

I like somebody! What now?

So you've started dating someone and you like them. You like them *a lot.* How soon should you stop dating other people?

First off, assume everyone is dating multiple people. No matter how nice or sincere someone seems about you, assume everyone, and I mean everyone, is playing the field and dating around. So if it's important to you that you date only each other — then it's time for The Talk. If you're afraid to bring up the subject of dating each other exclusively, then *trust your instincts and don't have The Talk yet!*

Let me just come right out with it: In the dating world, sex is a dividing line for many people. Even if you are hanging out every weekend and talking on the phone, texting, and emailing regularly, most people will assume that you are free to date other people — that is, until you have sex. Then everything changes.

I once saw an episode of *Seinfeld* in which the characters warned each other about this very situation. The idea was that you'd better think about the consequences before you had sex with someone because once you did the deed the other person was your girlfriend or boyfriend for a minimum of the next three weeks (any less time and you'd be considered a real schmuck).

The moral of the story is that if you jump into bed with someone on the first, second, or third date, that person may very well expect or assume that you are now officially in a relationship. I can't tell you how many times I've heard from people who inadvertently created a relationship that they now didn't really want — but felt obligated to be in — because they had become sexually involved. I therefore, encourage everyone to, if not discuss sex before having it, at least wait until you know the other person well enough to entertain the idea of being in an exclusive relationship with that person. And also, once a sexual relationship has begun, *always* discuss with the other person what this new development means. In other words, are you two now only seeing each other? While most people would assume so, it's vital to make sure that you are on the same page, because not everyone feels that sex equals exclusivity. (And there's nothing wrong with that.)

Besides sex, the other big relationship milestone that often gets conflated with the idea of exclusivity is the "I love you" declaration. Whether it happens during a casual conversation, in an intense talk, or during the heat of passion, it will make a big impression — positively or negatively.

Whether or not to enter into an exclusive relationship is, short of marriage, the most important relationship decision you will ever make. Therefore, don't make this decision lightly. Real life can be messy and you want to know that you've got a good partner during the hard times, as well as the good ones.

Remember my client Kate? Even though she was very attracted to and serious about her new man, she wasn't sure she wanted to be exclusive or even how to go about it if she did. In my book, she had the right attitude about not rushing into anything. After all, I have met many people who ended up in a monogamous relationship with the wrong person, which then segued into an unhappy marriage. After the inevitable divorce, they end up as my matchmaking or date-coaching clients.

Please also remember that The Talk should be separate from the question of sex. Many people conflate the two, and it's the cause of many tears and wounded hearts. So, don't rush into bed with someone and certainly don't stop accepting dates with other people until you've had the Talk and both of you have decided to be exclusive. I can't tell you how many people rush into sex and then feel obliged to be monogamous even though they barely know each other. Then, due to the level of physical intimacy, they convince themselves they're in love to justify being sexual and being together so soon. In fact, people often spend more time researching what car to buy or getting to know a prospective tenant than they do getting to know someone before they get sexual.

If you wouldn't trust someone with your ATM number or your email password, consider whether you should trust them with your heart. And if sex for you means that you'll give your heart to someone, don't rush into a physical relationship.

Looks Won't Make You Happy

I know of someone who divorced his wife because she didn't want kids, then he married again almost immediately to someone who had one kid already. He didn't want to be alone and she was hot. When his new wife decided she didn't want more kids, he then found himself in the same predicament as in his first marriage, except with a part-time stepchild. He ended up super depressed, several years older, and not sure what to do.

The One?

So you got through The Talk. You've been dating each other exclusively now for six months, a year, or much longer. Now how do you know if this person is your match? How do you know if this person could be The One? It's a really good question because a lot of times you meet people, you have a nice time dating, you go exclusive, but you're still just not sure if there's more potential there. What if you're dating somebody for a while, how do you know if this person could be the one to spend the rest of your life with?

Well… you don't. But I like to encourage people to think about how they *feel.* Don't think, analyze, or be overly logical. Is this person a match? Does this person have the things on my List? That's not what I'm talking about. Instead, give yourself some time to just really experience how this person makes you feel.

Do you feel energized when you think about seeing this person? Do you feel happy when you spend time with them? Do you look forward to speaking with them? If you're spending the rest of your life with somebody, God willing, you will have many years together. That's a lot of conversations and a lot of quiet time. You need to have a good physical connection and a physical attraction. Do you desire this person physically? Do you desire touching this person and having this person touch you? Do you share the same values and daily lifestyle? Do you have the same goals? Not everything has to be exactly the same, but the important things like values, goals, even just your daily rhythm matter a lot. Do you like to do the same kinds of things, eat the same sort of way, and share the same religious values and lifestyle, or lack thereof? That's what I would say are really the most important things in making lasting matches.

Is this person your best friend and your lover? While even your soul mate won't be all things to you, and never should replace your best friends, he or she should be right

How to Not Marry the Wrong Person

Don't marry someone because you're impressed by:

- What they do for living
- How much money they have
- Who their family is
- Where they live
- What their social circles are
- How attractive they are
- What degrees they have
- What universities they attended
- How much you love their kids
- How much you love their dog? Cat? Iguana?

You're marrying them. Not their family, friends, bank account, degrees, or social status. Too many people marry for the fantasy of the life they imagine; for status, for a fancy lifestyle, or because of sexual attraction. All of that gets old after a while and none of those things are enough to make a deep, soulful match.

up there with your besties. That's really what you want to look for in a match. Communication is the most important element of any relationship. You really need to talk things out and make sure you are on the same path, at the same point in your life and where you want to be.

Not **The One**

Be honest. Are you just in love with the idea of being in love? Or are you simply "ready to settle down" and have kids? Or are you madly physically attracted to your guy or girl, but just aren't that interested in them otherwise? None of these issues will go away with time. Given enough time, the current cracks in your relationship will emerge as major fault lines as big as the San Andreas.

On the more extreme end, are you turned off by something about them physically or their natural smell? Are you lonely when you're with them or when you think of a future life with them? Are you low on energy when you're getting ready to see them, and not excited when they call or email? Are you constantly annoyed by them, and dreading the idea of having a good chunk of time with them (like on a vacation)?

Please don't get seduced by looks. Everyone gets old and wrinkly eventually (it beats the alternative), and physical attraction won't sustain you long term. Make sure you have what *matters* in common.

Warning: Just Don't!

Don't marry someone just because she's pretty or sexy or you have great sex.

Don't marry someone because he checks all your check-boxes on your List.

Don't marry someone because it's time to "settle down."

Shouldn't you get married or commit to another person because you've found that one special individual you're in love with; your best friend and soul mate with whom you share meaningful goals and values, and not because you've turned a certain age, think it's time to get married, your parents want you to, or want to have kids? Take a long, hard look at your own motivations before you promise a lifetime to another person.

The devil you know

It can be tempting to turn a passionless date into a relationship or stay in a bad relationship or one going nowhere, since dating can be exhausting. Your subconscious mind tells you this is as good as it gets, don't expect real love, passion, or joy. Don't give up! Don't settle! Your soul mate is out there. As the title of the book *Better Single Than Sorry* urges, it's better to stay single than to be sorry and find yourself in a loveless marriage. Have faith that true love will come your way. You don't know what timeline your love has in store. But do know that when the timing's right, your soul mate will be there.

Your decision is yours alone

Why shouldn't you trust your parents' or friends' advice? Because there are two types of parents: Those whose child can do no right and those whose child can do no wrong. Yours is in the middle, you say? You're fortunate, but I still think most parents are so desperate to see you paired off or producing grandchildren that they aren't very objective as to why you should keep looking or commit. Plus, they aren't usually privy to the personal details of your relationships (like sex), so they don't have the complete picture and are often missing crucial details that are the reasons someone would or wouldn't be a good match for you. How many times have people told me that their parents constantly judge them for being unmarried or unattached, and hear "Why are you still single? at every family function?

As for your friends, the married ones are out of touch and either jealous of your freedom or wanting you to be as happy as they are and paired up, oftentimes at any cost. They aren't you, so they don't necessarily want the same life or type of person you desire, and they probably know very few single people, anyway, especially if they've been married a long time or have kids.

Negative Nellies and Nathans

Don't listen to your family and friends, especially the ones who are often negative about everything, always looking for the downside. It's easy for them to put down your prospective dates, they're not the ones sitting home alone on a Saturday night, and if they are, they want you to not have a date, either, so you can join them in their pity party. Remember, misery loves company — so avoid the miserable.

Movin' on!

Life's too short to waste on someone who isn't right. If your relationship partner doesn't treat you well or isn't a match, get out. If you were dumped and had your heart broken, you've already given enough time to this person who didn't appreciate you and clearly wasn't The One. How much more of your life are you going to give to a person who doesn't deserve it? Move on!

Why People Marry the Wrong Person and How to Avoid It

- Best friend, no sexual attraction
- Great sex, but no deep connection
- Pressure to settle down from family, friends, colleagues, or religious community
- Wanting kids before you're "too old" or everyone else is married

Questions to Ask Regarding Long-Term Compatibility

- Do you have kids, do you want kids? How do you plan to raise them?
- Are you messy or clean?
- How do you handle money — spending it and saving it?
- Do you believe in God? Are you religious? What holidays do you celebrate and how?
- How much time do you spend with friends and family?
- Are you a night owl or an early bird?
- What's your work schedule and what's your work-to-leisure-time ratio?
- What do you like to do on vacation and with whom do you travel, if anybody?
- What do you like to eat? Do you follow any special diet or have food restrictions?
- Do you have pets? How do you feel about different pets?
- How much money do you give to charity, if anything, and what types of causes do you care about?
- How do you like to spend your free time?
- What are your politics? How do you feel about people with different politics?

Note that these questions should be asked fairly early in the relationship, but there's no need to ask them all at once!

Get out there and date other people right away. I've met so many people who take months or even years to get over a broken heart when the person who hurt them immediately found someone else and is happily in a relationship, enjoying life. As I always emphasize to my clients, there's no better way to get over someone than to find someone better.

A Warning to Men

Don't be a mama's boy. Marrying someone to please your parents or not marrying to please them is a huge mistake. Furthermore, letting your parents get in the way of you and your spouse is a quick recipe for divorce.

One study by Queens College and the University of Illinois found that people who remained single for a shorter amount of time after a breakup recovered faster than people who waited a longer period to start dating again. Researchers surveyed a group of 313 adults, both single and in relationships, to discover how a "rebound relationship" really affects a person post-split. The study found that people with a new significant other claimed to feel more confident, in better psychological health overall, and (perhaps most significantly) claimed to feel a better sense of resolution to their past relationship.

That's not to say you shouldn't give yourself a few days of healthy breakup psychosis: Burn the gifts your ex gave you (except the jewelry), eat takeout straight from the container, dress like a modern-day Miss Havisham, and scream at the wallpaper. Then do some endorphin-boosting exercise to burn off the takeout pounds, wash your face, and find your rebound relationship!

Are you compatible?

What do people consider important? I personally don't have clients answer a million questions about themselves, but I do like to have them speak about some things that I consider really important. I like to know people's non-profit interests and whether they are into volunteering and charity. I also think about daily routines, like sleep schedules. Do you tend to stay up late and sleep in, or is it "early to bed, early to rise" in your house? I often hear from my divorced clients who aren't religious, that religion ended up being a much more important issue than expected, especially among those who have children. I also see diet as something people won't budge much on, whether it's those who won't give up fast food, those who keep kosher, those who are vegetarian or vegan, and so on. People into health food will find it tough to live with someone who's really into junk food, for example.

The best love matches come from similarity, not difference. It's as simple as that. Opposites are fun for the short term, but successful long-term matches share a lot in common — from daily lifestyle to deep-rooted beliefs and values.

As I've already said (repeatedly!) I try to encourage people not to be too set on height, age, weight, education level, or income — qualities that often get in the way of people finding a great match. Your true love may turn out to be a very different person than the one you imagined, so it's important to be open to the possibilities.

As financial advisor and author Suze Orman says, "you're not your credit score." You're also not your bank account, your car, your dress size, your genes, your parents' bad marriage, the insecure kid you were in junior high, or even the person you were in your bad marriage. At least I hope not. If you think you are, do your inner work on your own or with a good therapist, and get on with it so you can start finding the love you so want and deserve.

Do you think you're special?

Some people see their individual circumstances as barriers to getting into the dating game. Maybe it's their age, weight, being interested in someone before they are officially divorced, or other circumstances. Do not worry, these are not barriers to finding your soul mate. Let me share with you my experience with these situations.

The golden years

People often ask me what's the difference between dating for young people and dating for older people. Much to their surprise, I always answer "not much."

I have clients ranging from young adults in their 20s to seniors in their 90s. (Yes, I really do have a 90-year-old client — he's quite a catch and still drives!) Whether in their 20s, 40s, 60s, or even 80s, people are people. They seek love and companionship. Like everyone else, seniors are most likely to find it with people who share similar interests, intellects, lifestyles, values, and goals. That doesn't change with age.

Most prefer someone financially secure and healthy (though how that's defined varies), and certainly both health and financial status can change in an instant at any age. Perhaps older people are more concerned about finding a healthy partner, and some are more concerned about money (or less concerned if they are financially well off on their own), as they reach or are past retirement and possibly have more time to enjoy the benefits of a relationship.

The Pillbox Pitfall

As far as health goes, it's worth remembering that sometimes the smallest clues can have a lasting impact on a first date. Take the case of one of my clients, an elderly gentleman close to 80. He is a vibrant, fit, and healthy individual who prefers to date younger women. (When I say younger, I'm talking early to mid-60s, so it's quite a significant age difference.) He's pretty sure about his preference, and for good or for bad, he's really not willing to date women his own age.

In general, I usually tell people that you're more likely to find a compatible match if you date close to your own age. But that's not always what people want — especially men.

Take my client in his 80s who wants to date women in their 60s. I respect my client's wishes, and in this prerequisite he's adamant. I happened to know a woman who was in her early 60s, she agreed to meet him because she actually prefers older men, as long as the man is a lively, fit individual. Since this man played golf, and also liked going to the symphony and traveling, I thought they could potentially be a great love match.

She called me after her date to let me know that he took her out to lunch, and the first thing he did after sitting down at the table was pull his pillbox from his coat pocket. He started popping his premeal medications right in front of her! Of course, it's fine to need medication and to take medication; I'd wager that most individuals his age have a drug regimen. But — and this is big — if you're trying to present yourself as a healthy, youthful, fit individual, I don't think that pulling out your pillbox is going to make the best impression on a first date. (No, guys, it won't help to joke that you're taking Viagra!) Needless to say, she was put off by the pill performance and didn't want to see him again. For all I know, she's on a battery of medication too, but that's not really the point.

Whether it comes to your health, how much money you have, or how much education you do or don't have, you have to think about first impressions and what kind of impression you'd like to make. This goes for all of us of any age. When someone doesn't know you yet, they will use any tiny clue to conjure up a fantasy about you, good or bad. Those fantasies and first impressions can be notoriously difficult to undo. Plus, they invite further questions: Do you really want to share with a virtual stranger what pills you're taking, and for what?

Save yourself the headache. Excuse yourself to go "wash hands," and take your before-lunch pills in the powder room.

People are sometimes surprised to hear that I work with clients of all ages. But the fact is that companionship is important for everybody for mental health, for physical well-being, and for happiness in general. Companionship can certainly come from friends or family members, but some seniors — widowed, divorced, or lifelong bachelors and bachelorettes — are specifically looking for soul mate relationships.

As I mentioned earlier in the book, I used to work as a geriatric social worker with Holocaust survivors. At the nonprofit where I worked, I saw how those who had a loving partner to share their daily life did much better in all areas of their lives than those who were alone. I've seen for myself the benefits of romantic love for seniors, and I believe very strongly that people deserve to have love in their life at any age.

I'm also a big advocate of computer literacy for seniors. I think that seniors, who sometimes have decreased mobility or other health concerns that can foster social isolation, can especially benefit from being on social media and dating sites before meeting a date in person. However, it's still true that a surprising number of older people don't use computers at all, and many who do aren't comfortable using them for dating. And we've all heard horror stories of people (especially seniors) being targeted and taken advantage of both psychologically and financially by con artists on the internet. That's why I always temper my enthusiasm for seniors doing online dating with a bit of caution, and remember to repeat the usual advice to never ever give out personal information like Social Security numbers, addresses, and maiden names to people they meet online. Since dating sites are anonymous, you never really know who their users are or where they are located, so many older folks are understandably wary about engaging in online dating at all.

I often hear from these types of clients, those who want my personalized approach and expertise to screen and select matches for them. For those divorced or widowed seniors new to dating after many years married, they may be nervous or unsure of how to navigate the modern dating world, and they appreciate the personalized approach of a matchmaker who will also do date-coaching with them. (After all, some of my older clients haven't dated since the *Mad Men* era!) I do all matching and date-coaching myself (no staff or assistants answer my calls and emails or interview clients), so it's the ultimate in personal attention. It's like I hold their hand throughout the often intimidating dating process.

Others, because of who they are or their profession, don't want or can't have a profile on dating sites. Among my clients are doctors, therapists, rabbis, fire chiefs, educators and philanthropists known in the community. Of course, some people tire of the seemingly endless shallow players they find on dating sites. If someone is willing to take the time and spend the money to become my client, the thinking goes, they're much more likely to be genuine about finding love and a lasting relationship. (I find this to be true, most of the time anyway.)

Some of my older clients are less likely to try internet dating sites, but even that isn't the rule, especially in a computer-savvy place like the San Francisco Bay Area. As always, whether you are a senior looking for a mate online, offline, or using both, the most important thing is to keep hope alive.

For example, I recently matched two people in their late 60s who just got married. The match was really about the power of both of them having hope and faith and believing in love. He was a widower, and she had never been married. He desired and believed he could have a soul mate relationship a second time around, and she believed love was still out there for her.

It would have been so easy for her to adopt a litter of cats and enjoy tending her rose garden for the rest of her life (completely legitimate choices, I may add!), but she also desired a soul mate and believed she could have one. They both decided to act on their desires and beliefs by staying open to the possibilities and giving matchmaking a try. I love these two as an example of people who never gave up hope.

I notice that many people in their 40s tell me that they feel over the hill and like they're out of the game for meeting their soul mates. This makes me think of one woman, 90 years old, whom I recently met. Her husband of many years had died, and she was looking to date again. This man, whom she had been happily married to for 40 years, was actually her second husband. She told me that she divorced her first husband while in her 40s. He wasn't a nice guy, she told me — and she finally realized that she could be stuck with him for a quarter-century or more if her health held up! Even though she was afraid that she'd never meet anyone new and wasn't sure how she'd provide for her teenage children, she took a leap of faith and met the love of her life later that same year.

In contrast, when I was a social worker I had a 68-year-old client, a widow who felt lonely and isolated. She told me she wanted to meet a man, but admitted that she wasn't doing much to make it happen. She knew she had to get out there and try, since he wasn't going to just come knocking at her apartment door. My thoughts exactly!

So whether you're new to dating or an old pro, it's essential to have a positive attitude and get out there. You never know how, when, or where you're destined to meet your match. The important thing is to have faith, be open to make the most of the opportunities that present themselves, and enjoy your life in the meantime. You never know — love might find you in the process.

Also pertinent to the senior population, who are often on fixed incomes, is the advantage of the great financial perk of marrying or cohabiting. That is true simply because everything is less expensive shared by two. Whether it's splitting the rent, mortgage, or grocery bill, people have more disposable income to enjoy their golden years when they are part of a couple.

Another difference in dating for seniors is that many can't get married for legal and financial reasons such as wills, pensions, or Social Security. I don't require marriage as a goal for my clients, but just because you don't want to remarry doesn't mean that you shouldn't find love, and even move in together if that's what you desire.

As always, if someone chooses to be sexually active in a relationship, the same need for safer sex practices apply, as sexually transmitted diseases don't discriminate or pass over anyone based on age.

I'd say the main difference in dating for seniors is in the amount of dating and relationship experience people have. Some older folks have never married or been married multiple times, and come with an enormous amount of dating experience. (Think Rue McClanahan's character Blanche on *The Golden Girls*.) Others are newly divorced or widowed and haven't been on a date in more than 40 or 50 years. (That would be Rose Nylund, the Betty White character from the same show.) Dating can be nerve-wracking at any age, and the truth is that it takes the same effort and perseverance that looking for a job does (though it should be appreciably more enjoyable).

I'm one of the few matchmakers out there, especially in the Jewish community, to work with older people as much as I work with a younger clientele. I feel strongly that everyone deserves love at any age and love makes everything better. Finding a match isn't just about marriage and raising a family.

To that end, I charge less money up front and only more if I'm successful matching two people. And I don't make clients pay again and again every year, which is also unusual. I also stand by a policy of charging men and women equally. (Many services recruit men at singles events for no charge, since there are fewer senior men out there and the services often have quotas to meet a certain number of men for dates. I don't do that.) I only set people up when it's a genuine potential match, and I don't offer free or low-cost deals to men to farm them out for dating quotas. Not only do I find that practice dehumanizing to men — akin to "ladies' nights" at bars and clubs for young people — but also I find that men who are recruited to a dating service won't take dating as seriously if they had paid a fair, yet substantial fee for those services.

In other words, when it comes to dating services and apps, you really do get what you pay for up to a certain point. So far, I think I'm on the mark: Clients who used services that engaged in recruitment or too-good-to-be-true "specials" before meeting me often say it was a waste of time, being set up with many random men who obviously weren't an appropriate match.

The newly widowed

I often get asked: "Is it OK to date someone who is just recently widowed?" Of course it is, but you'll want to know what kind of state they're in.

Anyone who embarks on dating a widow or widower will have to be especially sensitive and empathetic to what they're hearing and seeing. Despite this, the potential payoff is huge. After all, we already know that a widow or widower is "the marrying kind" and has the potential to stick with a partnership for the long haul.

But what if this person is a very recent widow or widower, or was in an especially long and happy marriage? Shouldn't that person have time to grieve? Of course they should, but grieving is a very personal kind of process, and everybody's marriage is different. The timing of the death — a sudden death versus a death that was expected, where a person may have had 10 years of a long illness — makes a difference, as does the overall happiness of a marriage. Death affects everybody differently.

In Judaism, a person can actually go back out and find somebody to marry after just a few months of grieving. Although this may seem like a short time frame, I think it's because so many Jews have had to rebuild and rebound from tragedies and begin anew again and again. That's the way of the Jewish people. Although I have a lot of clients who are widowed or divorced, who aren't sure they can handle love again, they come to me because they really believe in their heart, deep down, that love really is what life's about, sharing your life with somebody. So there's a deep tradition there that encourages going through the effort of opening their heart up again.

Maybe, because a person had an especially wonderful marriage the first time around, he or she is really eager to get married or partnered again to somebody equally special, and why shouldn't that special person be you?

If you get involved with a widow or widower, just keep telling yourself that there are no hard and fast rules for grieving, and it's not up to you to decide how or how long someone else should grieve. Unless you were a close and personal friend of the couple — and even then! — you may not know the intimate details of the marriage. For widows and widowers, it's a very personal thing. Some people want to get out there right away and start dating. Other people take a few months or even years.

The important point here is that there are no rules. Each circumstance needs to be evaluated on its own. If you're considering dating a widower or widow, first listen to their feelings; don't impose on them your own ideas about how or how long they should grieve. More importantly, don't just listen to what they say: Actions speak louder than words. For example, do they tell you that they're ready for a new relationship but still have photos of their deceased spouse all over the house? If so, it's no reason to scream and run away, but it certainly demands a conversation.

For example, I had one client who was an intelligent professional in his early 60s. His wife had died after a decade-long illness, and he swore that he had mentally prepared for her death long before it actually happened. So I wasn't particularly worried when he came to me just three months after her death. However, when I learned how his first date went, I wasn't so sure.

No sooner had he and his date, a divorcee around the same age, sat down to dinner, he whipped out his smartphone. He proceeded to show her photos of he and his beautiful wife on vacation, at holidays, during family get-togethers. Perhaps this guy wasn't ready to move on, I thought to myself after hearing the woman's version of the evening's slideshow. So I called him up. After I spoke to him again, I realized he just was out of practice and needed a little date-coaching. That I could help with!

Dating somebody who is separated, but not divorced

Besides the question about widowers, the other question I get is: "Is it OK to date somebody whose divorce isn't finalized yet, or a person who is just separated from his or her spouse?" Again I would say YES. There are lots of reasons why people sometimes take a while to get divorced. Often it can be as simple as a financial thing, needing to wait to get health insurance or finalizing the details of custody arrangements for the children. Whatever it is, as long as your prospective date is sincere about moving on, being in a new relationship, and certainly not planning to reconcile with the former spouse or partner, I would say absolutely go for it!

Is your weight weighing you down?

I had one woman who came to me for matchmaking, and who had struggled with her weight all of her life. She had come to terms with the idea that she'd never be a Skinny Minnie, but she also knew from her past experience with online dating that most men would rule her out when they saw her size. The exact same day that she became a client, I interviewed another new client, a slim and trim version of her: They were in similar professions, had the same hobbies, grew up in the same neighborhood, and even had the same birth month and year. It was a wonder that they had never met until I set them up! I knew weight wasn't an issue for this man, and with all their similarities, they've been together ever since.

CONCLUSION

"It will never rain roses: When we want to have more roses, we must plant more roses."

— George Eliot

You only need one!

I know. Sometimes dating feels like a long slog through the cast of *The Night of the Living Dead,* but try not to become jaded. Fight the impulse to be negative and cynical about the dating pool. *Like attracts like.* Be positive and you'll attract a happy, positive person into your life. Visualize the kind of person you want to be with and the kind of life you'd like to lead. No one will want to join you if you're a party pooper and your life is a downer. Everyone has worries and difficult times to overcome, but your date doesn't need to hear about yours. You want to show you've got your act together. Show a potential mate how much fun it is to be with you, how nice a life with you will be.

Sometimes it feels like everyone's coupled off and there are no single people out there. Again, depending on the size of your community, it may be time for a change. The time may be ripe to try somewhere new, geography-wise, whether it's a new town or just a new neighborhood. Usually though, it's simply time to expand your circles. You'll discover there are many eligible singles out there, or certainly enough to keep you occupied for a while.

Remember, you only need one soul mate. It's that elusive one, which is so hard for some to find, on which you need to keep your focus. Don't waste time and precious emotional energy on dates you know are not for you, just to keep busy or avoid being home alone. There are plenty of meaningful ways you can spend your time: volunteering, exercising, or learning a new skill, rather than going out with anyone to fill your dance card. Be selective. Otherwise you may become bored, or worse, bitter and negative about dating. That attitude will project the wrong energy when the right one does come along. You never know who's going to cross your path and when it'll be that special someone. You want to be at your best and feel good when it happens.

You can do it! I know you can

What is a soul mate? Remember what I said at the beginning of this book: Your soul mate is truly your best friend and lover. Can you have more than one? Yes, you can. Can anyone find a soul mate if they really work on my steps ***Desire***, ***Believe***, and ***Act***? I firmly believe they can. I've seen it time and time again.

You can't will your soul mate to come to you exactly when you want, and you don't know at what point it'll happen in your life. So make the most of the time in between.

Again, you first need the *desire* to find your match. As I've said, because of societal or familial pressures, many people have bought into the idea that they need to be partnered regardless of knowing their true feelings. Not everyone wants to or needs to be partnered. And if you're just looking for companionship or sex or somebody to share your finances with, you'd be better off with a dog, a sex buddy, or a roommate to share your rent.

I have two types of clients: I guess you could call them the "glass half-full people" and the "glass half-empty people." The glass half-full people tell me they are "easy to match" (because they are so great!) and the glass half-empty people tell me that they are "difficult to match" — usually because of what they perceive as unsuccessful dating experiences in the past, but also sometimes because of their age, weight, what much of the world would consider a "disability," or some other characteristic. Rest assured, if for whatever reason you believe you are one of these difficult-to-match people, know your match is out there too. (In fact, you may be at a significant advantage over the "easy-to-match" people.) Case in point: I have a friend who found her match fairly late in life. They're incredibly in love, and have a plaque in their bathroom that says something along the lines of "Love is finding someone whose neurosis matches your own."

All kidding aside, while I have many attractive, successful, highly educated male and female clients of all ages, I always tell the ones that are concerned that whatever their perceived disadvantage or disability might be, when I have their match, it won't be an issue. And it truly won't. True love, the soul mate kind, doesn't care about your bank account, your need to use a cane when you walk, or that you dropped out of graduate school. When you find your soul mate, love is all that matters and the rest of the little details will work out.

Check your baggage and clear your blockages before trying to begin a new relationship. You need to truly *believe* that you can find your soul mate. Do whatever you need to do to get your inner self in its best shape and cultivate an open, fun, curious demeanor. Then work on all the outside stuff: Look your best. Get out and do things that help you meet other people and make you happy. Don't put your life on hold while you look for your special someone; it won't make you happy or project an attractive image.

I know it can be tempting to avoid the dating world and stay home and read a book, watch TV, or hang out with your cats or married friends rather than facing the singles scene. But again, you need to get out there to find love.

Above all, try to make dating fun. Think of it as an exciting adventure if you can. The story of your life and your happy ending are in process and it's going to be a surprise to everyone, including you, how the story turns out. Enjoy it. Take it all in, and most importantly, have faith your true love is out there.

Think of the boring dates, lonely nights, or broken hearts from relationships gone wrong as part of the experience of getting you to where and with whom you're supposed to be. The road may be long and bumpy or short and smooth. Everyone has different and unique experiences on their path to finding a soul mate. Once you and your best friend find each other, everything will fall into place, clearly worth the effort and hard times you went through to get there. You'll feel a joy, love, and peace of mind you've never before experienced in a romantic relationship.

Note that sometimes *geography* is the single biggest obstacle to two people meeting. I often have to convince a client in San Francisco to cross the bridge to date someone in the East Bay or Marin; same with people on the Westside of L.A. dating someone in the Valley. If you can be a little flexible regarding location, you really are at an advantage to finding your soul mate. As strange as it may sound, almost every match I made started out as a long-distance relationship. *If you are really in love, you don't stay long distance for long!*

Remember to call and not to text at the start so you can see if you like the sound of each other's voice and have a good rhythm in conversation. Texting is just so impersonal. You want to laugh together and see if there is any connection. And set up that date just as soon as you can. You don't want to invest time and energy or get emotionally attached before you meet and make sure there's some in-person chemistry.

OK, that's not necessarily true — I believe in love letters, after all — but it's something to remind yourself to make sure the meetup happens just as soon as possible. (Also remember that, if you're using an iPhone, which at least half of you are, then the recipient of your text conversation can see those ellipses when you start writing, change your mind, delete, and then start writing again.)

Know what you're going to say before you start a text. You want to project confidence and your best self in all your interactions. If you're not feeling it at that moment, you shouldn't go out or speak with a potential date.

If despite your best efforts and the advice in this book, you still feel very awkward about dating, consider hiring a dating coach. A good dating coach can not only help you with pre-date tips and post-date follow-up, but also he or she can help you screen potential candidates to eliminate the ones that aren't likely to result in a successful date or match.

While a matchmaker will do the heavy lifting for you in terms of finding a potentially compatible match, a dating coach can help you keep up your confidence as you navigate the dating world, whether you meet people through apps, friends, out in the world, or via a matchmaker. The advantage of getting a dating coach is that they're relatively inexpensive for those you can hire per session, but if you have the funds I definitely recommend a matchmaker as well.

Now go out there and find your match! Remember, you only need one. *I know you can do it.*

ACKNOWLEDGMENTS

The author wishes to thank Corrine Casanova, Liz Goodgold, Tanja Prokop, Randy Peyser, and Anthony Lazarus for their assistance in helping this book come to be. Gratitude also to S.W., Elizabeth Lissman, Christine Covey O'Neal, Reverend Susan Mills, Lynn Marceau, my mother Elaine Gottesman, Patti Breitman, Hope Bohanec, and Martin Rowe for their input and encouragement.

And to all the Gottesman dogs: Sparky, Mazal, Simcha, Malka, Tovah, Maya, Chico, Dakota, and Toby, who truly are "God's love manifested," as my father so perfectly told me.

About the Author

Judith Gottesman is a matchmaker and dating coach specializing in the Jewish community. The daughter of Rabbi Aaron Gottesman, who came from a long line of famous rabbis, she has always had an interest in the Jewish tradition of matchmaking and the idea that there is a soul mate out there for each and every one of us.

Judith began matchmaking informally more than 20 years ago, out of a desire to help others find love and happiness; she launched Soul Mates Unlimited® in 2009. Her technique, which employs equal parts psychology, attention to detail, and intuition, has resulted in many successful, lasting matches and marriages.

She has a undergraduate psychology degree from UC Berkeley and a master's in social work from Yeshiva University in New York City.

Other books by Judith Gottesman:
The Lost Art of Dating: A Dating Coach's Step-by-Step Guide to Finding Love at Any Age.

Contact Judith Gottesman at www.SoulMatesUnlimited.com or www.MyDatingCoach.co.

www.ingramcontent.com/pod-product-compliance
Lightning Source LLC
Chambersburg PA
CBHW060231030426
42335CB00014B/1403
* 9 7 9 8 9 8 5 0 9 1 1 0 6 *